Knitting
with Wire

Nancie M. Wiseman

INTERWEAVE PRESS
www.interweave.com

Technical Editor: Jean Lampe
Illustration: Gayle Ford
Photography: Joe Coca
Design: Dean Howes
Production: Dean Howes, Samantha L. Thaler
Copy editor: Stephen Beal
Proofreader: Nancy Arndt

Printed in China by Everbest Printing Company, Ltd.

Library of Congress Cataloging-in-Publication Data

Wiseman, Nancie, 1950-
 Knitting with wire / Nancie M. Wiseman.
     p. cm.
Includes bibliographical references.
 ISBN 1-931499-31-4
 1. Knitting—Patterns. 2. Wire craft. 3. Wire. I. Title.
 TT825 .W59 2003
 746.43'2—dc21
                              2002151328

10 9 8 7 6 5 4 3 2

Acknowledgments

My very first thank you must go to my husband Bill Attwater, who does all of the cooking, errands, and anything else I ask him to do, giving me time to play with all of these wonderful techniques. Your patience, encouragement, and kindness are dear to my heart as well as your presence in my every-day life. You are my joy.

Thanks to my brother and sister-in-law Charles and Dorothy Wiseman for your encouragement from afar. I know you're always out there sending me your love.

Thank you to the folks at Soft Flex® Wire Company for providing the Artistic Wire and tools for me to use for this book. Your generosity is greatly appreciated. Without people like you to provide us with wonderful products to inspire and encourage our designing, this "work" wouldn't be nearly as much fun.

To the folks at Interweave Press for giving me the opportunity once again to write a book for you—you are a joy to work with and I'm glad to be part of the "flock" once again. Thank you for your friendship and kindness.

Contents

Introduction

As I think back to how I got started knitting with wire, I remember my inspiration and my first project with great clarity. On one of my many teaching trips, I had purchased a bracelet at an art gallery in Wisconsin that I thought looked like it had been knitted. I used a magnifying glass to try to figure out how the artist had made it. It looked like I-cord or spool knitting, but actually it was links of wire made to look like it was knitted. Inspired by this, I said to myself, "Why can't I knit with wire?"

At this time, my only source for wire was the local hardware store. I walked into the store, asked for the wire department, and tried to answer the question "What do you need it for?" without sounding silly. In fact, I don't think I answered at all. I purchased a couple of packages of 18-gauge copper wire and went home to experiment.

Now, I ask myself, "Why didn't I start with something easy?" Nope, not me, I was jumping in with both feet. My first project was a bowl that I began on four double-pointed needles. Yikes, what could I have been thinking? Fortunately it worked out well enough that I was willing to "soldier on," as my husband would say, with more projects. The copper wire was the worst feeling stuff to knit with and the bowl feels like you could use it to scrub the oven. But, the lessons I learned from knitting the bowl were invaluable: You

can drop a needle out of the knitting and it doesn't matter; you can't drop a stitch. You have to knit loose and use lots of hand lotion to save your fingers. And finally, I had to find better wire and in smaller gauges.

Once I got the hand knitting with wire under control, so to speak, I began experimenting with other wire knitting techniques. Viking knitting, which is used to make jewelry and sculpture, doesn't even use knitting needles, but it looks like knitting and looks so fabulous that I wanted to master it as well. My research and how-to information on Viking knitting is included here with patterns and directions.

Finally, machine knitting with wire was the final step in my research and exploration of wire knitting. It's also included. The patterns and directions for these projects might even inspire you to buy a knitting machine, if you don't already have one under the bed.

That's how I got started knitting with wire. I highly recommend you try some of the simpler projects until you get the "hang" of it. In case you're looking, I haven't included the directions for the first bowl I knitted, because I don't want you to know how really crazy I was to knit it in the first place.

Have fun and enjoy every project. Good tools, good wire, and good beginner choices are the key, and they are all explained inside.

Tools for Working with Wire

Generally speaking, the better your tools, the more you'll enjoy working with wire. Economical versions of all these tools are available, but after you've worked with wire for a while, you'll probably want to invest in more precision equipment. Please don't bring out those greasy old cutters and pliers from your garage to use with your fine and beautiful wire. They probably won't have smooth blades for even cutting, and they're too clunky to work with.

Bead stores, craft stores, and even some hardware stores sell wonderful tools for reasonable prices. You will need to buy some of the tools or supplies from a hardware store, because they are made specifically for furniture building or plumbing; I'll let you know which ones they are.

Wire Cutters

Also known as Flush Cutters. In general the wire gauges used for knitting with wire are within the cutting range of a good pair of high-quality jewelry cutters. Most cutters will have a flat side for smooth cuts and an angled side for sharp cuts. The cutters should also have a comfortable grip in your hand. The blades should be very sharp and smooth. Never use the cutters to cut anything but wire. If you are cutting a large amount of heavy-gauge wire from 18 gauge or below, you may want to consider a heavier pair of cutters.

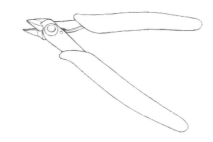

Pliers

Round-Nose: These pliers are essential for creating and rounding loops. They should have a fine smooth point. Because the tips are larger toward the handle, various size loops can be made with the plier. It should have a comfortable grip shaped to one's hand.

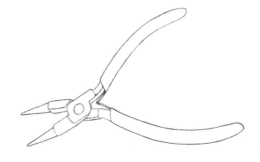

Flat-Nose: Used for gripping the wire while working it into a shape. They should be smooth and without teeth, which would mar or scratch the wire. Also used for pulling Viking knitting through a draw plate.

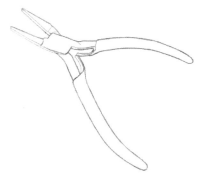

Chain-Nose: A plier that resembles a needle-nose plier, but is more useful in wire working because there are no teeth to ruin the wire. Used for crimping down the ends of wrapped wire and for working in small areas. Can also be used for pulling Viking knitting through a draw plate.

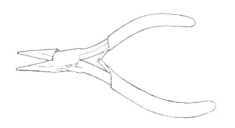

Wire Smoother: This specialized tool has a nylon-covered jaw to smooth wire or to grip wire with absolutely no destruction to the wire's finish. Used with all wires, but especially with fine wires when hand knitting due to the constant twisting and turning. Good tool to use with Viking knitting also, to straighten the wire that is bent with every stitch.

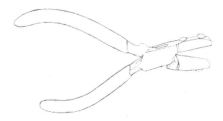

Specific Tools for Specific Techniques

Tools for Hand Knitting

General Knitting Supplies: Think of what you would normally carry in your knitting bag: markers, stitch holders, measuring tapes and safety pins. They aren't always necessary, but can be useful when needed.

Knitting Needles: Wood or bamboo needles work very well with wire, and I prefer them. The warm feel of the needle with the cool feel of the wire helps the knitting flow better. The wire will turn the ends of a light-colored wooden needle dark, but the color will not come off on yarn. Metal needles feel like the wire is "scraping" across the surface. Plastic needles can get grooves in them if the wire is worked too tightly. Most of the knitted projects don't require a lot of stitches, so short double-pointed needles work very well.

Small Zip Lock Bag: To keep the wire from tangling, use a small plastic bag with a zip lock to hold the wire as you knit; in this way the wire will flow smoothly instead of becoming a wad of kinks that resembles a "Slinky" that is impossible to straighten.

Tools for Viking Knitting

Allen Wrenches (also known as Hex Wrenches): Used as a mandrel, this L-shaped tool is commonly found in hardware stores. It has six sides, with gentle angles to assist with stitch formation. They come in a variety of sizes both metric and English. Available in black and sometimes in silver, the wrenches come in sets or individually. If you purchase a set be sure you can get the short end of the wrench into a vice. Allen wrenches are easier to work with than

knitting needles or dowels; it is difficult to get the wire under the old stitch to make a new stitch on the rounded knitting needle or dowel because the old stitch lies flat against the surface.

Allen wrench

Drawplate: A drawplate is normally used to make wire. This metal plate has tiny holes that metal is extruded through to create the wire. The wooden drawplates used for Viking knitting are similar, but have larger holes. The holes resemble the holes on a knitting needle gauge. When I first started working with Viking knitting, I couldn't find

Drawplate

4

a drawplate, so I marked a hard piece of wood using the holes on the knitting needle gauge and had a friend with a drill press create the drawplate for me. Number the holes on the drawplate with a pen, making the largest hole number 1 and the next smaller sizes 2, 3, 4, etc. These numbers can be used as a reference when you make matching pieces. These numbers will also be referred to in some of the patterns.

Small Pointed Tool: Used to open up stitches or to help in viewing where a new stitch is to be made. Using the tip of the tool, you can move the wire slightly, straighten it or pull it out so the new stitch is easier to make. Use a small metal file, a fine crochet hook, or a size 1 or 2 (2.25–2.75 mm) metal knitting needle.

Tools for Machine Knitting

Standard-Bed Knitting Machine: There are a variety of brands of this type of machine. A basic machine is all that is needed. The ribber is not used. The wire will not ruin the machine.

Accessories: These generally come with the machine. If you don't already have them, you can purchase them from machine knitting stores or websites. You will need the following:

Claw weights, at least 2

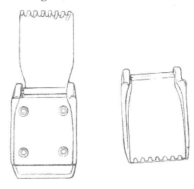

Transfer tools, a 1-3 and a 2-3

Latch or tappet tool

Tapestry Needles: Size 18 or 20 tapestry needles, and general use sewing needles used for grafting stitches, sewing items together, and weaving in ends.

Small Box, about 2 inches (5 cm) deep. I use a checkbook box. Cut small half circles into the narrow ends to fit the dowel.

Use a ¾-inch (2 cm) dowel that will fit the width of the box and will hang slightly over the edge, and will fit into the half circles made in the box. The dowel does not turn; only the wire on the dowel turns.

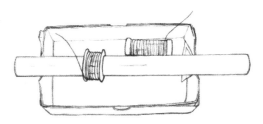

Tools for Making Findings

"Findings" are clasps, jump rings, loops, and hooks that you can make or purchase. You may want to try to make some of your own because handmade findings are a good match for items that you've made yourself. If you purchase findings, be sure you get high quality metals and sturdy clasps or closures.

Knitting Needles: Used to make round objects such as jump rings and loops for clasps. In general, an 8, 9, or 10 (5, 5.5, 6 mm) needle will work for most purposes. Needles can be made of any material. These tasks are a good use for knitting needles that have lost their partner.

Small Hammer: A variety of sizes and weights of hammers are available from both bead stores and hardware stores. A small ball-peen hammer from a hardware store works great. It should weigh about 6 to 8 ounces (170–227 g). Used to flatten and harden handmade findings.

Small Anvil or Steel Bench Block: Used for hammering the findings you make from wire; wire becomes harder when pounded. Be careful when you're hammering metal on metal to keep the surface of the wire from marring.

Small Piece of Suede: Used for hammering wire findings when the wire has crossed over itself. The wire will break very easily when pounded too hard where it crosses itself. Covering the object with the suede will help eliminate the breakage.

Choosing the Right Wire

We can now choose from a wide range of wire in many sizes and colors. When I started working with wire, I bought 18-gauge copper wire from the hardware store. It was awful, but when that's the only choice, it works just fine. Now you'll have so many choices it will be difficult to make up your mind. In the Projects sections, I've given appropriate sizes of wire, knitting needle, or Allen wrench to use. You will find that, depending on your individual technique, some pieces may come out slightly smaller or larger. For the most part such variance is not critical because the object doesn't have to "fit" like a sweater would.

For colored wire I use Artistic Wire. It comes in a wide range of colors and sizes. The wire is a very good grade of copper with a permanent color coating. I have had very few problems with the coating coming off the wire, even though I have manipulated it many times in the knitting processes. Using the wrong tools can "dig" into the color and leave the copper underneath exposed.

When you're using the colored wire make sure to purchase enough for a project. Believe it or not, wire has a dye lot and the color you order today may not match the same color you order a month from now. There is no dye lot number given as there is with yarn, and the wire dye lots vary, enough to make the color differences apparent. So purchase all the wire for each project at the same time and avoid dye lot problems.

Fine jewelry wire, of course, is the ultimate to work with for any of the techniques. Silver, sterling silver, gold, copper, or brass can yield the most beautiful results. Don't dismiss the gold- or silver-plated wires; they will wear well and look beautiful for a very long time. Some of the gold- and silver-plated wires come wrapped in a large circle or loop and the ends are secured with tape. Be sure to secure the end of the wire after cutting, otherwise it will become a tangled mess that you will have to cut to untangle. For machine knitting, the wire must be on a spool, so wires packaged such as these cannot be used for machine knitting.

The finer jewelry wires also come with a designation of "hardness": half hard, dead soft, and hard. This scale is derived from the process of heating the wire to strengthen and harden it. For knitting projects in this book, you'll find that half hard and dead soft work just fine. Dead soft is quite easy to work with and will make jewelry that is very soft and malleable, good for the Viking knitting technique. Half hard is generally the most commonly used wire.

Jewelry wire also comes in shapes: square, half round, and round. You'll find the most pleasing effect from using the round wire. Even though the half round looks beautiful, it has a tendency to twist and the stitches will not look even.

Wire Sizes

The gauge of the wire is the wire's diameter, the higher the number, the finer the wire. Use the following gauges for the specified techniques when you start to experiment on your own:

16 to 20: for findings, and embellishments

20 to 28: for hand or Viking knitting

32 and 34: for machine knitting. With wire any heavier you run the risk of ruining the machine.

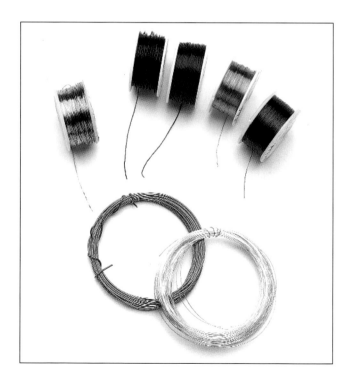

How to Make Findings

Many of the projects in this book require some sort of clasp, closure, or finding. I encourage you to use your imagination when you're making your own findings. Don't be afraid: The wire is strong and will tolerate a lot of stress. If you make your own findings instead of purchasing them they will match the knitting perfectly because many of the wire colors are available in both the finer and heavier gauges (see Tools for Making Findings, page 6).

When making findings cut pieces about 6 to 8 inches (15–20.5 cm) long. Don't use lengths that are too long and impossible to work with. The more you work with wire the easier it will be to estimate the lengths of wire to cut. Depending on what I'm making, I tend to use wire no longer than 6 to 10 inches (15–25.5 cm) long. You may find that you have to make an object more than once to get it just right. The correct tools are essential to keep the wire from getting scratched or marred in any way (see Tools for Working with Wire, page 2).

Caution: I strongly recommend that you wear some sort of eye protection when you're cutting wire. Little bits and pieces can fly everywhere. I do all of my cutting over a small trash can so I can be sure the ends are contained when they're cut. Be careful if you have small children, animals, or significant others who walk barefoot; the little ends are sharp and can easily get lodged in the carpeting.

Jump Rings: An essential part of connecting any finding or object to a knitted project. One critical thing to remember about jump rings is they must be opened from the side, not by enlarging the circle.

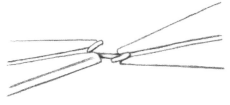

Opening jump rings

If you open your jump rings carefully, they will remain strong and hold together for a long time. Jump rings are generally made from heavier wire, 16 to 18 gauge, and can be hammered slightly to harden.

Knitting Needles: Knitters already have these tools to make jump rings; they're perfect for wrapping the wire around and are available in many sizes.

To Work: Wrap the wire around the knitting

9

needle, keeping the loops as close as possible and all the same size (Figure 1). Wrap a few more loops than required in case they do not come out evenly or you lose one. The first and last wrap with the tails will not make a loop. Cut the wire from the spool. You can pound the loops lightly while they are still

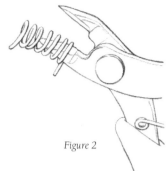

Figure 2

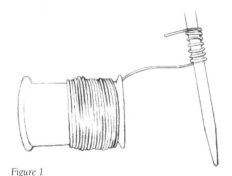

Figure 1

open, perfect for joining them to whatever you're making. You probably won't need to open them anymore, just slide them through the objects they are attaching (Figure 3) and gently squeeze shut with flat-nose or chain-nose pliers. If you need to open them further,

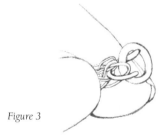

Figure 3

on the knitting needle to harden them.

Remove the set of loops from the knitting needle. Using the angled edge of the wire cutters, cut the jump rings apart (Figure 2). Because I'm right handed, I hold the loops in my left hand and make a loose fist around them so that when I cut them apart they don't fly away.

When the rings are cut they will be slightly

gently open from the side as little as possible.

"S" Hooks: Hooks work well as clasps on necklaces or bracelets.

To Work: Cut a piece of wire about 3" (7.5 cm) long and straighten. Using the round-nose pliers, make a loop about 1" (2.5 cm) from the end of the wire; the end of the wire should cross over the middle of the wire (Figure 1). Trim where it crosses

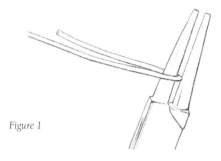

Figure 1

the working wire, leaving about ⅛ to ¼" (3–6 mm). Curve the other end of the wire the opposite direction into a tight circle using the round-nose pliers (Figure 2).

Figure 2

Repeat for the other end, in the opposite direction, making the second loop about half the size of the first (Figure 3). Hammer gently.

Figure 3

Wrapped Hook and Eye: This hook is very strong and does not require jump rings to attach to an item.

To Work Hook: Cut a piece of wire about 3" (7.5 cm) long. Make a loop about 1" (2.5 cm) from the end using the round-nose pliers (Figure a). Bend the tail of the wire at a right

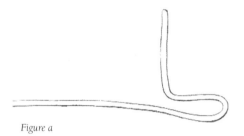

Figure a

angle about ½" (1.3 cm) from the bend. Wrap it around the base of the loop (Figure b). Trim the opposite end so it is just long enough to be woven into the piece of jewelry

Figure b

for about ¼" (6 mm) and fold back against the wrap made with the other end of the wire (Figure c, page 12). Bend the loop into a hook (Figure d, page 12).

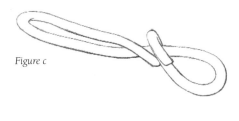

Figure c

Wrapped hook and eye

Figure d

Eye: Repeat as above, making a larger loop at the beginning by wrapping the wire around a size 8 to 10 (5–6 mm) knitting needle (Figure e). Fold second tail up to wrap (Figure f).

Scrolls: These wonderful curls of wire are strong, fun to make, and very decorative. They can be made large or small, square or in shapes, with the wire close together or far apart.

To Work: Cut a piece of wire about 4 to 5" (10–12.5 cm) long. Straighten. Using the round-nose pliers, make a loop with one end of the wire (Figure 1). Continue bend-

Figure 1

Figure e

Figure f

ing the loop until it touches the long end of the wire. Using the chain-nose or flat-nose pliers, grip the loop tightly and continue to turn the wire tightly around the center loop. It should be a flat spiral (Figure 2, page 13). Continue moving the pliers and turning the loop until it is the correct size; hammer gently.

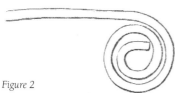

Figure 2

Scrolled Hook and Eye: This closure is similar to the type of hook and eye you can purchase for sewing. It will be attached with wire in the same manner as the purchased hooks: Sew the scrolls down and then sew across the base of the hook.

To Work Hook: Cut a piece of wire about 5 to 6" (12.5–15 cm) long. Make a scroll at one end about ¼ to ⅜" (6 mm–1 cm) diameter (Figures 1 and 2). Bend the wire about ¾" (2 cm) from the end of the scroll into the hook (Figure 3). Work scroll to

match for other side. Gently hammer; bend long loop into a hook (Figure 4).

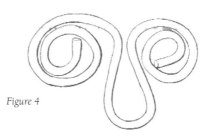

Figure 4

To Work Eye: Cut wire to about 4 to 5" (10–12.5 cm), work same as Figures 1 and 2, except at the end of the first scroll, Figure 2, bend the wire to leave a flat eye for catching the hook (Figure 5).

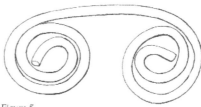

Figure 5

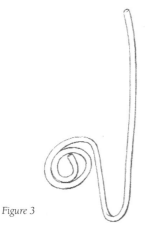

Figure 3

Finished scrolled hook and eye

Hand Knitting with Wire

I have not been able to discover when or where hand knitting with wire began, but this technique is probably very old. Certainly the Viking knitting technique dates back many centuries and, since metal has historically been a choice material for making jewelry, it stands to reason that at some point hand knitting with wire probably was used for making belts, headpieces, or jewelry.

Arline M. Fisch, author of *Textile Techniques in Metal*, has been knitting with wire for several years and in her opinion any wire or metal can be used in traditional textile techniques. I agree! Knitting with wire will broaden your horizons and give you new "fiber" to experiment with. The process and the tools are much the same, so you'll be familiar with the steps before you even get started.

You will use the same steps for working with wire as you do for general knitting but they will feel slightly different because the wire doesn't stretch like yarn. You won't need to worry about making your knitting smooth and even because it's pretty near impossible. Knitting with wire feels like play. You'll find you have to knit looser and even somewhat sloppily when you're working with wire. If you knit too tightly, you won't be able to get the needle into the stitch for the next rows. Pulling too tightly on the wire

or wrapping the wire through your fingers will also be hard on your hands. I use extra lotion on my hands to keep the wire moving smoothly with little distress to my manicure or my fingertips.

Before you start knitting with a spool of wire, place the wire in a small plastic zip lock bag. I use a bag about 3 by 4 inches (7.5 by 10 cm). The spool should be able to roll in the bag. Bring the end out through the top and zip the bag shut except for the small area where the wire is coming out. This system will prevent the wire from tangling as it comes off the spool. You can place the bag in your lap or on the floor and just let the wire flow from the bag as you need it.

When you're knitting with wire be sure to pull down on the knitting every row or two. The wire will not fall down and off the needle as yarn does because it doesn't have any weight. If you don't pull the knitting down gently it will get caught right under the knitting needle and it will just sit there and make knitting the next row impossible.

When you're finishing off the wire, cut with the flat side of the wire cutters toward the knitting so you don't get a sharp point. To weave in the wire always try to work it into the side that will not be against your skin or clothing. The wire will not pull out as yarn does so you don't need to weave in as you would with a sweater. For jewelry, you can generally hide the wire where the clasp is attached. Cut the ends flat. If they are too sharp use an emery board to sand the point into a flat surface. Be careful not to expose the copper by sanding the color off the sides. **Note:** When directed to sew or bury the ends, use the wire as though it were a needle. You won't need sewing or tapestry needles unless they are listed in the supplies.

If you need to start new wire in a project, twist together the end you're dropping and the new end and just keep knitting. The ends can be taken care of later. In general you'll find that most of the projects in this book are worked without having to add new wire. Fortunately, you won't find knots in wire, but you may find kinks. Use the wire smoother to straighten them. They don't need to be perfect; you won't notice them after they're knitted. If you overmanipulate a kink, you will likely break the wire.

And finally, one of the best parts of knitting with wire: Once you've knitted a stitch it's done. It won't unravel. You pull the knitting needle out and the stitches will be there when you come back. In fact you don't need stitch holders, but if they make you feel more confident, I've listed where you can use them in the pattern directions.

Casting On: I have created a new cast on, the Wire Cast On, abbreviated WCO. I use it with some of the heavier wires, 20 to 26

gauge, because a long-tail cast on is too difficult to work with the stiffer wires.

Using same size needles planned for the project, hold both needles together in your left hand to make the cast on very loose so you can easily knit the first row. Remember the wire doesn't stretch like yarn.

Take the wire and fold it over the needles, leaving the 12 to 20" (30.5–51 cm) tail toward the back and the working wire from the spool toward you.

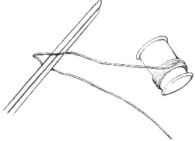

*Bring the tail toward you on the left side of the working wire. Wrap the tail around the front of the working wire and toward the back.

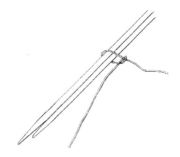

Now move the working wire toward the back and over the top of the needle toward you.

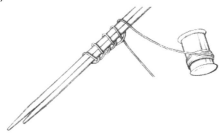

Repeat from * for desired number of stitches. Wrap the tail around the working wire twice on the last stitch. Remember: Keep the wire loose on the needles.

Remove one of the needles and begin knitting.

Two options for casting on with work in progress:
Knit-On Cast On: Loosely knit into an existing stitch; don't drop the stitch off the left needle and move the new stitch from the right needle to the left needle, keeping it loose. Repeat for desired number of stitches.

Backward-Loop Cast On: Hold the wire in your right hand and wrap it over your left thumb and around so it crosses over itself. Insert the knitting needle into the loop on the thumb and pull off. Do not pull too tightly. Repeat for desired number of stitches.

Increases: I generally use a Yarnover for an increase. The wire won't stretch enough to work a knit in the front and back of the stitch or a Make One increase. It is possible to use these increases but they put a lot of stress on the wire. When you use a Yarnover always knit into the back of it on the next row to close up the hole. In some cases you'll see it's not necessary, because the knitting already has holes, so what's one more?

Decreases: There is no need to work mirror image decreases. In fact the easiest decrease to work is slip 1, knit 1, pass the slipped stitch over (sl 1, k1, psso). It doesn't show and it doesn't require the wire to stretch as much as knitting two together or slip, slip, knit does. This decrease can be used at either end of the knitting.

Binding Off: For most of the wire the normal binding off technique works. That is: knit 2 sts, *pass the first stitch over the second stitch on the right needle and drop it off the needle. Knit one more stitch and repeat from * until all sts are used. Finish off.

If you find the wire you are using is too heavy and the stitches are too bulky with this technique, you can knit a stitch, take it off the right needle, twist it a couple of times, and fold it over the edge of the knitting. Repeat across the row, alternating the sides the stitch is folded over. Another good method is to cut the wire and run it through the stitches on the needle and finish off.

To Place Beads: In the directions, you will be told to knit a bead row. To do this you must have all of the beads prestrung on the wire. When you're instructed to work the row, knit the first stitch, *place a bead next to the knitting, and knit the next stitch. Repeat across from *. The beads just sit on the wire between two stitches; they do not get knitted into the stitch. The beads will be on the side of the knitting away from you when this row is worked.

To Place Beads at the Beginning of the Row: Prestring the beads on the wire. At the beginning of the row, move a bead(s) up to the edge of the knitting and knit the stitch. The bead will sit on the wire coming from the previous row as you work the first stitch of the next row. These beads are not knitted in to a stitch. You can manipulate the wire a little if the bead falls into the first stitch. It should sit on the outside edge and jiggle slightly.

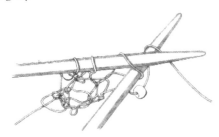

Hand Knitting Projects

Note: For any of the instructions that direct you to place beads, see the how-to section in the Hand Knitting with Wire chapter (page 17). All hook and eyes or closures that are not purchased are described in the How to Make Findings chapter (page 9). Refer to this section for directions on how to attach findings when the information isn't included in individual project instructions

Purple Beaded Bracelet and Necklace

Terrific beginner project and fun to work with beads.

Sizes

Bracelet length: 7½" (19 cm).
Necklace length: 20½" (52 cm).

Materials

Artistic Wire, 28 gauge, silvered lilac, 1 spool.
Artistic Wire, 18 gauge, silvered lilac, about 12" (30.5 cm).
Size 2 (2.75 mm) knitting needles.
Size 8° seed beads, color to match, ½ tube.

Bracelet

String about 100 beads on the 28-gauge wire. CO 5 sts. At beg of every row, slide 2 beads down next to the knitting and knit across. When piece measures 7" (18 cm) or desired length, BO. Using 18-gauge wire, make a wrapped hook and eye (see How to Make Findings, page 9). Attach hook to one end of bracelet and the eye to the other end, centering them in the middle of the cast-on and bound-off edges. Finish off ends.

Necklace

Note: The necklace will curve on the side where the beads are placed. It is not supposed to be a straight piece. The curve is to fit around the neck.

String about 180 beads on the 28-gauge wire. CO 5 sts.

Row 1: Place 2 beads at the beg of row and work as for bracelet.

Row 2: With yarn in back, sl 1 kwise (see Abbreviations, page 88), knit to end. Repeat these 2 rows until piece measures about 20" (51 cm). BO. Using 18-gauge wire, make a wrapped hook and eye (see How to Make Findings, page 9), and attach the hook to the upper end of the cast on and the eye to the bound off edge. Finish off ends.

Pink and Purple Square Basket

Simple garter and stockinette stitch make this unique two-color basket a good beginner project.

Size

7 × 7 × 4" (18 × 18 × 10 cm).

Materials

Artistic Wire, 26 gauge, fuchsia—main color (MC), 2 spools; purple—color A, 1 spool.
Artistic Wire, 18 gauge, fuchsia, 3 yards (2.75 m).
Size 5 (3.75 mm) knitting needles.
Basic Tools.

Note: Side 1, base, and side 2 are made in one continuous strip.

With MC wire, CO 20 sts. Knit 2 rows. Work in St st until the knitting is square. Sample shown is 4½" (11.5 cm). Change to color A and work garter stitch for the same length as MC section. Change to MC, *work St st until slightly shorter than first side. Knit 2 rows. Cut wire, leaving a 20" (51 cm) tail. Weave tail through stitches on knitting needle. Fold stitches over wire*. (See Binding Off in Hand Knitting with Wire, page 14.)

With right side facing, using color A, pick up 20 sts across edge of purple base, work from * to *. Repeat for other side.

Using MC wire, whipstitch (see Glossary, page 87) the 4 corners together.

Corner Pieces: Using round-nose pliers and about 24" (61 cm) of 18-gauge wire, make a large square section for the top (see illustration). Hammer slightly (be careful not to hammer the knitting), and weave the end of the wire through the knitting at the seam. Cut wire leaving enough to make a small square at the bottom. Gently hammer the small square, and bend it outwards to make a "foot." Repeat for all corners.

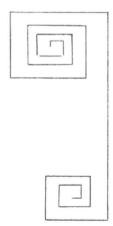

Woven Basket

Simply knit strips woven together for a perfect beginner project.

Size

About 4 × 4 × 4" (10 × 10 × 10 cm).

Materials

Artistic Wire, 26 gauge, silvered plum—
  color A; silvered peacock—color B; sil-
  vered blue—color C, 2 spools each color.
Artistic Wire, 16 gauge, navy, 24" (61 cm).
Size 4 (3.5 mm) knitting needles.
Size 9 (5.5 mm) knitting needle.

Sides and Bottom

Make 3 strips in color A and 3 strips in color C as follows: WCO (see Hand Knitting with Wire, page 15) 6 sts. Knit until piece measures 16" (40.5 cm). BO, and finish off by cutting wire and threading tail through last stitch. Make 2 strips in color B as follows: WCO 8 sts. Knit until strip measures 16" (40.5 cm). BO, finish off.

Construction

With size 9 (5.5 mm) knitting needle and navy 16-gauge wire, make 12 jump rings (see How to Make Findings, page 9). Weave the bottom together following diagram A for color placement. Pull each strip up to form spokes for basket sides and attach each strip to adjoining strip with jump rings. Weave the horizontal strips through the side spokes beg at lower edge (diagram B). Using the wire, sew side pieces together after they are woven. Finish off. Adjust woven strips so basket will stand up evenly.

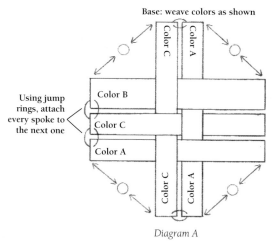

Base: weave colors as shown

Color C — Color A

Color B

Using jump rings, attach every spoke to the next one

Color C

Color A

Color C — Color A

Diagram A

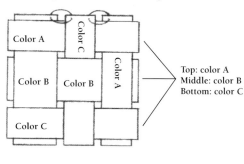

Sides: weave side band colors as shown, starting at bottom and work to top

Color A

Color C

Color B Color B

Color A

Color C

Top: color A
Middle: color B
Bottom: color C

Diagram B

Mini Beaded Cardigan and Pullover

Every knitter needs one of these simple sweaters to wear as a pin or place on their desk.

Size

3 × 5" (7.5 × 12.5 cm).

Materials

Artistic Wire, 28 gauge, magenta for cardigan; green for pullover, 1 spool each color.

Size 8° seed beads in contrasting colors, about 85–90 to sew on neck edge, borders, and sleeve cuffs.

Size 2 (2.75 mm) knitting needles.

Note: Knit-on CO, see page 16.

Cardigan

Back: *CO 16 sts. Work garter st for 2" (5 cm).

Sleeves: Loosely CO 8 sts at the beg of the next 2 rows, using knit-on method—32 sts. When sleeve measures 1" (2.5 cm) divide for neck: **Right Front:** Working across the first 13 sts only, work a yo inc at the neck edge every other row 3 times*. Cont with 16 sts until sleeve measures 2" (5 cm) from sleeve CO edge. BO 8 sts at sleeve edge. Cont in garter st with remaining 8 sts until side seam measures 2" (5 cm). BO.

Left Front: With RS facing, rejoin wire at neck edge, BO 6 sts very loosely for back neck, knit across row—13 sts. Work as for right front reversing shaping. BO remaining 8 sts.

Pullover

Work from * to * of cardigan directions. After neck increases are completed for right front, cut wire and rejoin at neck edge, BO 6 sts, knit across row. **Left Front:** Work on 13 sts as for right front reversing shaping at neck. After 3 incs are completed, on the next WS row, work across 16 sts of left front and join to right front by knitting across the remaining 16 sts. When sleeves measure 2" (5 cm), BO 8 sts at beg of next 2 rows. Continue working on remaining 16 sts until side seam measures 2" (5 cm). BO.

Finishing for Cardigan and Pullover: Using wire tails when possible, whipstitch (see Glossary, page 87) the side and underarm seams together. To place beads around neckline, cuffs and borders, attach a long end of wire to the knitting, string a bead on the wire and whipstitch to the edge. Evenly space the beads, stringing on a new bead every time a stitch is made.

Copper Sock and Mary Jane Shoe

Show your love for knitted socks and a matching shoe—an intermediate project.

Sock

Size

4½ × 5" (11.5 × 12.5 cm).

Materials

Artistic Wire, 26 gauge, natural, 2 spools.
Size 3 (3.25 mm) double-pointed needles, set of 5.
1 stitch holder; waste yarn to use as marker.

Note: The sock should fit tightly into the shoe for the set to stand up. The wire can also be shaped to make the sock fit in the shoe.

WCO (see Hand Knitting with Wire, page 15) 36 sts, divide sts equally over 4 needles. Join, being careful not to twist the CO. Work circular St st for 3½" (9 cm).

Divide for heel flap: K9 sts on needle #1, turn work, p9 sts, and then p9 sts from needle #4. Working on these 18 sts only (place rem 18 sts on holder for instep), work flat, back and forth in St st for 2" (5 cm), ending with a knit row. *Turn heel:* (WS) P11 sts, p2tog, p1, turn. Sl first st, k5, ssk, k1, turn. *Sl first st, purl to within one st of gap between the sts created when work was turned, p2tog (using one st from each side of the gap), p1, turn. Sl first st, knit to one st

before gap, ssk (using one st from each side of gap), k1, turn. Rep from * until all sts are worked, ending with a knit row—12 sts.

Gusset: With loose needle and RS facing, pick up 7 sts along left side of heel flap (needle #1); with needle #2, knit across 9 of the instep sts on holder; with needle #3, knit across rem 9 instep sts; with needle #4, pick up 7 sts along right side of heel flap, then knit 6 sts to center of heel sts. Insert waste yarn into next st to mark beg of rnd. Slip rem 6 sts onto needle #1.

Rnd 1: Needle #1, K13; knit across 9 sts each on needles #2 and #3; needle #4, k13. A total of 44 sts.

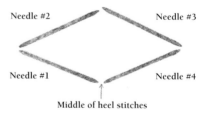

Needle #2   Needle #3

Needle #1   Needle #4

↑
Middle of heel stitches

Gusset Shaping:

Rnd 1: Knit.

Rnd 2: Needle #1, knit to last 2 sts, k2tog; needles #2 and #3, knit across all sts; needle #4, ssk, knit to end of rnd. Repeat these 2 rnds until 32 sts rem.

Slip 1 st from needle #2 onto needle #1, and 1 st from needle #3 onto needle #4— you should have 8 sts on each needle.

Continue knitting until foot measures 3" (7.5 cm) from heel.

Toe Shaping: Needle #1, knit to last 2 sts, k2tog; needle #2, ssk, knit to end; needle #3, knit to last 2 sts, k2tog; needle #4, ssk, knit to end of rnd.

Rep this rnd until 12 sts rem. Knit to end of needle #1 then slip 3 sts onto needle #4; slip 3 sts from needle #3 onto needle #2. With 6 sts on one needle for top, and 6 sts on another needle for the bottom, graft toe sts tog using wire and Kitchener st (see Glossary, page 87). Finish off. Fold about ½" (1.3 cm) down at top of sock for cuff.

Shoe
Size
5 × 3" (12.5 × 7.5 cm).

Materials
Artistic Wire, 26 gauge, black, 1 spool.
Size 7 (4.5 mm) knitting needles.
Size F/5 (3.75 mm) crochet hook.
1 bead or small button.

Note: Since there is no stitch gauge, your shoe may be slightly different from the size shown.

Sole: WCO (see Hand Knitting with Wire, page 15) 8 sts. Knit 2 rows. Inc 1 st at beg of the next 4 rows—12 sts. When sole measures 4" (10 cm) from CO edge, dec 1 st at the beg and end of every other row until 4 sts rem. BO. The sole should be about equal to the bottom of the sock if you want to place the sock in the shoe.

Sides: WCO 5 sts. Knit for 4" (10 cm). Inc 1 st at beg of every other row 4 times—9 sts (center front of toe cap). Dec 1 st at beg of every other row 4 times to reverse shaping. Be sure decs are made at the same edge as the incs were. Knit for 4" (10 cm) or to match opposite side. Do not BO. Cut wire, leaving about 6" (15 cm) tail. Weave back seam together with wire tail, sewing sts from knitting to CO sts.

Using wire, whipstitch (see Glossary, page 87) the sole to the shoe sides, lining up the center back and center front. Pinch the seam after it is sewn, so there is a definite line between the sole and the body of the shoe. With RS facing and starting at the left edge of the shoe where the strap will be attached, work a row of single crochet (see Glossary, page 87) around the top edge of the shoe, join with a slip st, do not finish off, continue with strap: crochet a chain of 24 sts, turn work, single crochet in 3rd stitch from hook (buttonhole) and in each chain across. Join to edge of shoe with a slip st. Finish off. Weave in all ends. Use wire to attach bead or button on opposite side of the shoe.

Note: All directions remain the same to make a left shoe except: Begin the crochet for the strap on opposite side of the shoe.

Asymmetrical Sculpture

Diagonal-type knitting for an advanced wire knitter.

Size

3 × 3" (7.5 × 7.5 cm).

Materials

Artistic Wire, 26 gauge, blue, 1 spool.
Size 4 (3.5 mm) knitting needles.
Glass beads, ¼ to ½" (6 mm–1.3 cm) in diameter, assortment of blue and turquoise, about 75–80.
Safety pin or waste yarn to use as marker.

Prestring beads on wire in random order and color. WCO (see Hand Knitting with Wire, page 15) 3 sts.

Row 1: (RS) Knit. Mark this as RS with pin or waste yarn.

Row 2: Pull a bead up to the edge of the knitting and knit across row.

Row 3: K1, yo, knit to end. Knit into the back of yo on the next row.

Repeat Rows 2 and 3 until there are 12 sts.

Row 4: Work as Row 2—10 beads in place.

Row 5: Pull a bead up to the edge of the knitting, k1, yo, knit to last 2 sts, sl 1, k1, psso (see Abbreviations, page 88)—12 sts. (This is the bottom edge.)

Knit into the back of yo on the next row. Repeat Rows 4 and 5 until the bottom edge has 14 beads.

Row 6: Work as Row 2—upper edge has 24 beads.

To shape opposite end:

Row 7: (Decrease row) Pull a bead up to the edge of the knitting, knit to last 2 sts, sl 1, k1, psso.

Row 8: Knit to end.

Repeat Rows 7 and 8 until 2 sts remain. BO. Cut wire leaving 20" (51 cm) tail, and thread through last st.

Using tail, whipstitch (see Glossary, page 87) the diagonal edges together. Sew beads over the seam to the lower edge and then back up the opposite side of seam to match. Beads should meet at the top edge.

Bottom

WCO 8 sts. Knit 8 rows. Inc 1 st at each end of the next 2 rows by working a yo. Knit into the back of each yo on following row. Knit 2 rows. Dec 1 st at each end of the next 2 rows by working sl 1, k1, psso (see Abbreviations, page 88). Knit 8 more rows. BO. Cut wire, leaving a long tail. Use wire tail to sew the base into the bottom of the sculpture, easing the base to fit.

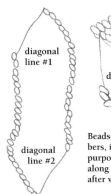

diagonal line #1

diagonal line #2

diagonal line #2

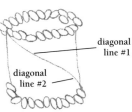

diagonal line #1

diagonal line #2

Beads not shown in exact numbers, illustration for placement purposes only. Attach more beads along diagonal lines #1 and #2 after whipstitching seam together.

Black Pearl and Multigem Bracelet and Necklace

Small needles, small wire, and beautiful gems and pearls—a perfect intermediate project.

Sizes

Bracelet length: 7½" (19 cm) with clasp.
Necklace length: 21" (53.5 cm) with clasp.

Materials

Artistic Wire, 34 gauge, aqua, 1 spool.
Multigem Chips, amethyst, citrine, and peri-dot, 1 strand.
Freshwater Black Pearls: 7.5 to 8 mm barrel shape, 1 strand; 5 mm round shapes, 1 strand; 12 mm elongated shapes, 1 strand.
Size 1 (2.25 mm) double-pointed needles.
Size 10 beading needle.
For Bracelet: One bar clasp about 1" (2.5 cm) long and ¼" (6 mm) wide, 8 jump rings in silver color. All findings are purchased.
For Necklace: Hook and eye clasp about 1½" (3.8 cm) long and ½" (1.3 cm) wide and 2 jump rings in silver color. All findings are purchased.

Thread wire through beading needle and randomly string chips and pearls. Use more chips in random colors between the pearls to keep them separated.

Note: The wire will break if the needle is left in the same place throughout the stringing of the beads. After every 2" (5 cm) of beads or so, move the needle to a new position on the wire. Cut off the used wire that was bent and ruined from the bead needle.

Bracelet

(takes about 220 pearls and gemstones)
CO 6 sts.
Row 1: K1, *drop the first gemstone or pearl down next to the knitting, k1*; rep from * to * across row.
Row 2: Knit. Repeat these 2 rows, randomly using 2 gems instead of 1 every third or fourth row. If the pearls are falling too close together, using the gemstones at a faster or slower rate will adjust the placement. When bracelet measures 7" (18 cm) or desired length, BO.

Finishing: Using the end of the wire, sew on the bar clasp to both ends. For extra reinforcement use jump ring to attach the bar clasp too. Insert the jump ring through each hole in the clasp and into a secure place in the knitting. Weave in wire ends.

Necklace

Using the remainder of the gemstones and pearls strung on the wire, CO 2 sts. *K1 st, drop the first pearl or gemstone next to the knitting, k1. *Do not turn.* Move wire toward you under the knitting needle, drop another gemstone or pearl down next to the knitting, slide the knitting to the right end of the knitting needle; repeat from * for length of necklace, approximately 20" (51 cm). BO. Use jump rings to attach clasp. Weave in wire ends.

Ebony and Ivory Collar

Lots of seed beads on fine wire make this unique collar. An intermediate project.

Size

26" (66 cm) long × 1½" (3.8 cm) wide.

Materials

Artistic Wire, 34 gauge, black, 1 spool.
Artistic Wire, 26 gauge, black, 12" (30.5 cm), for hook and eye.
Size 8° seed beads, cream, 8 strands.
Size 0 (2 mm) knitting needles.
Tapestry or sewing needle; plastic bag.

Tie together the wire and the thread of strung beads and gently push the beads over the knot and onto the wire. Retie a new knot further up the wire for each strand of beads, cutting off the used wire. Push the beads down the wire. Keep the wire strung with beads in a plastic bag as you knit to keep it from tangling. With 34-gauge wire, CO 15 sts.

Row 1: Knit.
Row 2: K1, *place a bead next to the knitting, k1*; repeat from * to * across row.

Repeat Rows 1 and 2, working shaping on Row 1 as follows: Sl 1, k1, psso, (see Abbreviations, page 88) knit to 1 st from the end, yo, k1. Knit into back loop of yo on next row. When work measures 13" (33 cm), ending with Row 2, reverse shaping working as follows: Row 1: K1, yo, knit to last 2 sts, sl 1, k1, psso. Row 2 remains the same. When second side equals same length as first side, end with Row 2. BO loosely. With 26-gauge wire, make a scroll hook and eye closure (see How to Make Findings, page 12). Using 34-gauge wire, attach findings to upper points at center front. Weave in all ends.

Red Beaded Purse

Garter stitch and beads make this unique and fabulous purse. Advanced project.

Size

About 9" (23 cm) in length × 7" (18 cm) wide at the widest section.
Measurements do not include beaded fringe or purse chain.

Materials

Artistic Wire, 32 gauge, red, 1 spool.
Bag Lady purse frame number BL80G in Polished Brass, with 1 yard (91.5 cm) of chain and 2 rings to attach chain.
Fabric for lining, red, ¼ yard (23 cm) 45" (114.5 cm) wide.
Lightweight iron-on interfacing, white, ¼ yard (23 cm) 22" (56 cm) wide.
Size 5° triangular beads, gold with red lining, 4 pkgs—0.62 ounces (17.58 g) per pkg.
Size 8° triangular beads, gold with red lining, about 58 beads.
Size 8° seed beads, gold, about 160 beads.
Silamide beading thread to match lining and beads.
Size 1 (2.25 mm) knitting needles.
Sewing needle.
Size 10 beading needle.

Pre-string 5° beads with 32-gauge wire, CO 14 sts.

Row 1: Knit.

Row 2: K1, *place a bead next to the knitting, k1*; repeat from * to * across row.

Repeat these 2 rows, *and at the same time,* work a yarnover one stitch in from each end of the next row, and then every fourth row until there are 30 sts. Knit into the back of the yarnovers on the following row. Work even on 30 sts rep Rows 1 and 2 until piece measures 4" (10 cm) from CO edge. Dec 1 st each end every other row (Row 1) until 2 sts remain. BO. Work second piece the same.

Note: Lining should be cut to fit the measurements of your purse, which may not be the same measurements as sample purse.

Lining

Maintaining a ¼" (6 mm) seam allowance, make a paper pattern to match your purse frame and knitting (see schematic on page 38 for shape).

Using your paper pattern as a guide, cut 4 pieces of lining. Then cut 2 pieces of interfacing without the seam allowance. Pin interfacing to the wrong side of 2 lining pieces, and iron on to attach.

For both sets, with RS together, sew around the top of an interfaced lining piece together with a plain lining piece. This is the section where the purse frame will fit the purse opening. Clip corners of both pieces to sewing line; avoid cutting through stitches. Turn right side out, press.

Flip the lining piece without interfacing out of the way and sew the two lower inter-faced body pieces together. Tuck the top of the purse lining out of the way and, with RS facing, sew the two plain lining body pieces together leaving an opening at the bottom to turn the lining right side out. Clip all corners. Turn entire piece right

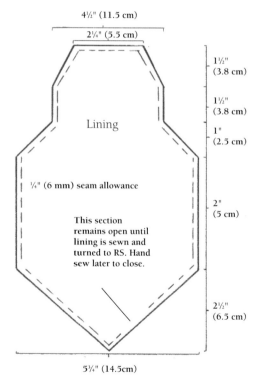

4½" (11.5 cm)

2¼" (5.5 cm)

1½" (3.8 cm)

1½" (3.8 cm)

Lining

1" (2.5 cm)

¼" (6 mm) seam allowance

2" (5 cm)

This section remains open until lining is sewn and turned to RS. Hand sew later to close.

2½" (6.5 cm)

5¼" (14.5cm)

Measurements shown are those of lining for sample purse, measure your knit purse and frame to determine exact meas-urements before cutting lining.

sides out through opening. Press seams. Hand sew the opening closed.

Hand sew the lining to the inside of the frame, placing the interfaced pieces of the lining facing toward the WS of the knitting. With Silamide thread and sewing needle, stitch the lining pieces to the purse frame using the attachment holes in the frame; sew through each hole in the frame. Then sew the knitted wire to the outside of the frame using the same holes, and catching the lin-ing at the same time.

Sew on 5° red/gold triangle beads to the outside of frame to cover the holes.

Fringe

With Silamide threaded on beading needle, secure thread to lower edge of purse then string fringe beads as follows: alternate a small triangle bead and a gold bead 7 times, then place a small triangle bead, a large tri-angle bead, 2 gold beads, 1 large triangle, and 2 gold beads. Re-insert the needle through the previous large triangle bead and cont through the remaining beads on the strand. Stitch fringe to the lower edges of purse catching both the lining and the wire each time fringe is attached. Work 14 fringes on each side and 1 in the middle.

Use rings to attach chain to purse frame.

Viking Knitting

I first read about Viking knitting in Irene From Peterson's book *Great Wire Jewelry, Projects and Techniques* (see Resources). I was intrigued by the fact that some of the finished pieces looked knitted even though few of the tools used to make the jewelry were what one normally carries in a knitting bag. The process for creating the pieces was completely different and totally fascinating.

I'm always interested in new techniques and new ideas so I immediately purchased the appropriate tools to try the Viking knitting technique. I had already been experimenting with hand knitting with wire, had made several projects, and had begun teaching the technique. I was beginning to get a complete picture of all the wire knitting techniques available.

Although I've changed some of the ways the techniques are worked in Peterson's book, I have basically followed her guidelines. But, I have taken the technique and expanded it to make not only jewelry, but also sculpture and vases covered with Viking knitting.

After mastering the technique I was very curious about its origin. Where did it come from? How did it get its name? It was a bit difficult to research the technique but here is what I found. I hope you find it as fascinating as I do.

Peterson notes that the technique originated in Scandinavia, where evidence shows that the Vikings had the technology to make wire chains. The importance of these chains is that solder was not used to hold them together—they were linked together to form supple and flexible chains. The Vikings used primitive forms of the tools we use today, but they were able to create both very heavy and very fine chains.

The Vikings created both jewelry and woolen clothing using the same technique, now known as Viking knitting. It is thought this may have preceded traditional knitting. The finished product has a similar look to knitted I-cord or the tubes of knitting produced by spool knitting. The one main difference in the appearance of Viking knitting versus regular knitting is that the stitches are twisted as though you had knit into the back of a stitch.

Many have compared Viking knitting to nålbinding. This technique uses yarn and a yarn needle to make loops that are joined together by "sewing" a single loop into a previously made loop that resembles the handwritten letter L. The process is different from Viking knitting in that nålbinding has a "cast-on" edge to start from and Viking knitting feels like you are working backwards from the cast-off end. The finished products also look and feel quite different.

Bishop Richard Rutt, in his book *A History of Hand Knitting*, found evidence of fine and decorative work resembling knitting in the Byzantine world and evidence that it was probably derived from Greek work done in the millennium before Christ. Similar work was also found in the city of Trichinopoly (or Tiruchirapalli) near Madras in South India. Trichinopoly is also a name used to describe Viking knitting.

Of course it doesn't matter what we call the technique or how old it is. It's pure fun, and it creates beautiful metal jewelry or sculpture. Now, let's get to the projects and how to make them.

Viking Knitting How-To

You won't use traditional knitting supplies to work this technique. Here is a list of the supplies you will need to get started:

26- to 28- gauge wire.

Small amount of scrap wire in a different color in the same gauge wire used in the project.

Allen wrenches (also known as hex wrenches). The sizes for each project are listed in the patterns. Generally ¼ to ⅜" (6 mm–1 cm) in diameter, Allen wrenches are used because the angles on the wrench ease the insertion of wire under a stitch.

Small bench vise, about 1–2lbs (454–907 g),

or a vise that can be securely clamped to a table or work surface.

Wire cutters.

Wire smoothers.

Ruler, or piece of stiff cardboard, 1" (2.5 cm) wide.

Drawplate (see Tools, page 4).

Getting Started

Directions are given for right-handed with (left-handed) directions in parentheses.

Viking knitting has to be started from a bit of wire shaped like a flower and known as a Startup Bundle or Bundle. The bundle behaves like a provisional cast on in regular knitting and is removed when the project is completed. Bundles are made with waste wire left over from other projects.

The bundle or "flower" needs to have as many "petals" as you want to work stitches for the project. The project instructions specify how many petals are required; much the same as knitting instructions indicate the number of stitches to cast on.

Using a ruler and waste wire, wrap the wire around the ruler as many times as necessary to form the number of loops or petals required for the project (Figure 1, page 41). Cut the wire and wrap around the base of the bundle (Figure 2, page 41). Create the flower by separating the petals away from each other so they resemble an open flower (Figure 3, page 41).

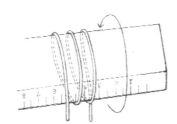

Figure 1

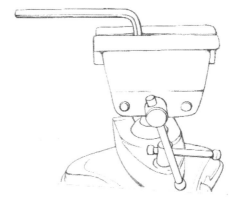

Figure 4

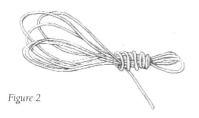

Figure 2

Place the short end of the appropriate sized Allen wrench in the vise with the long end toward the left (right) (Figure 4).

Cut a piece of the working wire about 24 inches (61 cm) long, and wrap one end around the base of the bundle over the waste wire wrap (Figure 5). Place bundle petals over the end of the Allen wrench and hold the bundle in place with the left (right) hand (Figure 6, page 42).

Figure 3

Figure 5

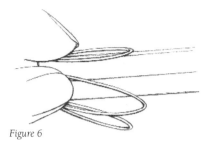

Figure 6

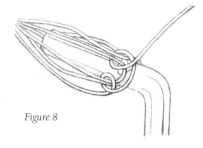

Figure 8

The petals of the bundle will now get connected with the working wire. Insert the working wire under the wires of two adjacent petals from back to front. The wire should come out and toward you over the end of the working wire connected to the bundle. Pull the wire toward the right (left) to make a loop that resembles the letter "e" around the two wires of the petals (Figure 7). The new wire should be crossing over itself. Continue around the bundle, turning the bundle toward you as you join the 2 sides of adjacent petals in the same manner (Figure 8). If you have 4 petals you should have 4 stitches; if you have 5 petals you'll have 5 stitches.

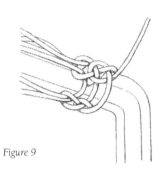

Figure 9

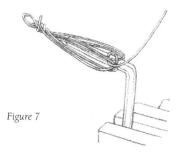

Figure 7

Working around the Viking knitting, always turning it toward you, go under the previous stitch where the working wire crossed itself (Figure 9). Keep the stitches similar in size and separated from each other the same distance as much as possible. It can be difficult to keep the rows straight; use the small pointed tool to help you move stitches and rows to keep them aligned.

TIP

- The drawplate will straighten this all out if you have difficulty keeping the stitches in perfect alignment.
- Keep the wire smooth; if a kink occurs, use the wire straighteners to smooth it out. Do not work with the wire kinked, because it can cause breakage later.

If you need to remove the work from the Allen wrench to straighten wire or trim a rough edge, do not crush the tube or work stitches without putting the tube back on the Allen wrench. The Allen wrench is there to support the work and keep it the same size throughout the process. The knitting should be moved or taken off the Allen wrench a little bit at a time; only about ½" (1.3 cm) needs to be on the wrench while working. The knitted tube will hang off the wrench as it is completed. Do not crush.

Joining New Wire

When the working wire is about 1 to 2" (2.5–5 cm) long, or you can't hang onto it anymore, join new wire in the following manner. Cut the old working wire to about ½" (1.3 cm) and leave it lying on top of the Allen wrench away from the stitches (Figure 1). Cut a new piece of wire about 24" (61 cm) long and make a hook in one end with a ½" (1.3 cm) tail. Insert the tail under the stitch you just finished, but this time, insert it away from you. *This is the only time you will insert wire away from you instead of toward you.* Bring the ½" (1.3 cm) hook over the tail of the old wire and twist slightly. Hold your left (right) thumb over the two wires and make the next stitch in the next column of stitches (not the same stitch used to join wire). This step will anchor the tails (Figure 2). Each time you come to the tails,

Figure 1

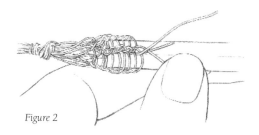

Figure 2

work the stitch in the normal manner, but also go under tails as well. This process is similar to knitting in the ends in traditional knitting.

Note: You cannot add more knitting to the Viking knit tube after it has been drawn through the drawplate. It is always best to overestimate the amount of knitting to work before drawing it through. Any excess knitting can be trimmed off later. One can work small gauge samples and write down how much they enlarge after drawing through. This will be a rough estimate because the more knitting there is the longer it will grow. You can depend on the tube growing at least 20 percent, but it will probably be more.

To Draw Viking Knitting through Drawplate

Place the drawplate in the vise and secure. You can hold the drawplate in your hand, but it is easier to draw through the Viking knitting if the drawplate is stable and you can insert the knitting without having it move. Take the end with the waste wire still

attached and insert it from back to front, toward you through a hole on the drawplate that is about the size of the knitting. Using flat-nosed or chain-nosed pliers, pull the knitting through the drawplate with one smooth motion. Insert the knitting into the next smaller hole and draw through again. Continue drawing through smaller and smaller holes until the knitting is the required length or you like the feel of it.

Note: You must always draw the knitting through the drawplate using the end with the waste wire.

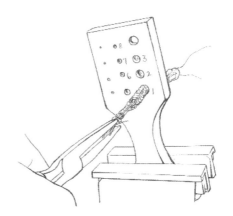

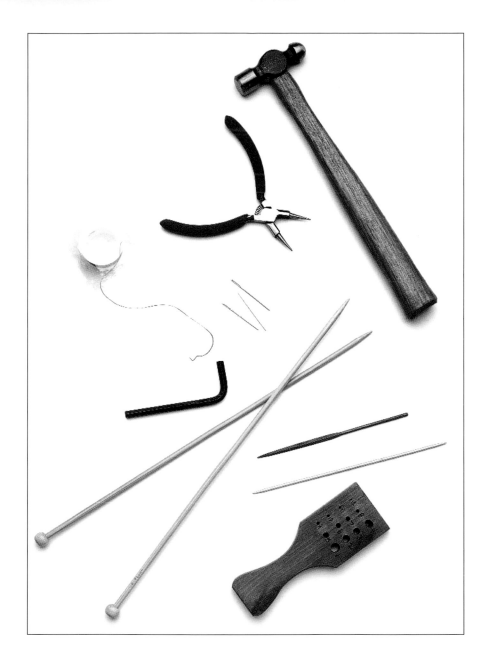

Viking Knitting Projects

Autumn Leaves Necklace

Basic Viking knitting with beads and glass leaves for embellishments.

Size
Length: 21" (53.5 cm) with clasp.

Materials
Artistic Wire, 28 gauge, natural, 1 spool.
Artistic Wire, 18 gauge, natural, 24"
    (61 cm), for jump rings.
¼" (6 mm) Allen wrench.
Waste wire, 28 gauge, contrasting color,
    ½ yard (46 cm).
Drawplate.
Basic tools.
37 rondelles (large-hole bead that looks like
    a donut) or spacers.
3 large glass blown leaves.
10 small glass leaves with metal loop at top.
Lobster claw clasp, ¾" (2 cm).
Size 6 (4 mm) and 8 (5 mm) knitting
    needle, 1 needle each size.

Abbreviations
R = rondelle without a leaf
RS = rondelle with small leaf
RL = rondelle with large leaf

Using the basic Viking knitting setup (see Viking Knitting How-To, page 40) and 28-gauge waste wire, start with 5 loops. Join the natural 28-gauge wire and work the chain for about 12 to 13" (30.5-33 cm). Draw chain through drawplate to approximately 20" (51 cm) in length.

With 18-gauge wire and size 8 (5 mm) knitting needle, make about 50 jump rings (see How to Make Findings, page 9). With 18-gauge wire and size 6 (4 mm) knitting needle, make 2 small jump rings. Using larger sized jump rings, connect leaves to the rondelles. Thread rondelles on the necklace from the beginning of the chain (the end you drew through the drawplate).

Threading order:
2 R, 1 RS, 2 R, 1 RS, 1 R, 1 RS, 2 R, 1 RL, 2 R, 1 RS, 1 R, 1 RS, 2 R, 1 RL, 2 R, 1 RS, 1 R, 1 RS, 2 R, 1 RL, 2 R, 1 RS, 1 R, 1 RS, 2 R, 1 RS, 2 R

Finishing: Remove waste wire, weave ends of working wire to inside of tube. Attach 1 small jump ring with lobster claw clasp to one end of necklace, and one small jump ring with a large jump ring to the other end.

Necklace with Large Bead

Another great way to embellish basic Viking knitting.

Size

Length:18" (46 cm).

Materials

Artistic Wire, 26 gauge, silvered plum,
  1 spool.
Waste wire, 26 gauge, contrasting color, 12"
  (30.5 cm).
1 Glass Orchid or large bead.
2 small silver jump rings, purchased.
2 small coils with end loop, purchased.
1 silver S clasp, purchased.

Using basic Viking knitting setup (see Viking Knitting How-To, page 40) and 26-gauge waste wire, start with 4 loops. Join silvered plum wire and work chain. Finish chain at about 12" (30.5 cm). Draw through drawplate so the chain is small enough to fit through hole in bead, about the 5th or 6th hole on the drawplate. Place bead or glass flower on necklace after drawing through. Cut away waste wire.

Finishing: Pull each end of knitting through a coil; be sure it is secure. Place a jump ring and the clasp loop on the left end of necklace, place a jump ring and S clasp on the right end.

Double Wire Viking Knitting with Pendant

An unusual glass piece used with Viking knitting incorporates two pieces of wire.

Size
Length: 20" (51 cm).

Materials
Artistic Wire, 26 gauge, green, 1 spool; purple, 1 spool.

German Silver Wire, 18 gauge, 24" (61 cm).

Waste wire, 26 gauge, contrasting color, ½ yard (46 cm).

Decorative glass piece with wire loops at the top.

⅜" (1 cm) Allen wrench.

Size 8 (5 cm) knitting needle.

Drawplate.

Basic tools.

Using the basic Viking knitting setup (see Viking Knitting How-To, page 40) and 26-gauge waste wire, start with 4 loops. Join both colors of 26-gauge wire, and hold together as one throughout. Work 12" (30.5 cm) of chain. Draw chain through drawplate using the smallest hole possible. The resulting tube of knitting should measure 18" (46 cm).

Trim off waste wire. Weave ends of working wire into center of tube. Using 18-gauge wire for both ends, wrap the ends of the tube for about ½" (1.3 cm). Turn two wraps out so they hang down. Make two S hooks (see How to Make Findings, page 9) with 18-gauge wire. Close one S hook tightly. Leave the second one slightly open so it can be used as the clasp. Hammer flat. Using the size 8 (5 mm) knitting needle and 18-gauge wire, make 4 jump rings. Connect 2 jump rings to the ends of the knitting and the remaining 2 jump rings to the loops on the decorative glass piece. Connect the closed S hook to the jump ring at the end of the knitting and then to the jump ring on one end of the glass. Connect the open S hook to the opposite side, making sure that it will go over the jump ring.

Note: If the decorative glass piece has one loop at the top or you are using a large bead instead, and creating a loop with wire, make the Viking knitting slightly longer and attach both ends to the loop at the top of the bead.

Heavy Viking Knit Gold Bracelet

Use thicker wire to create a heavier bracelet to really show off your skills. Intermediate.

Size
Length: 8" (20.5 cm).

Materials
Gold-filled Wire, 20 gauge, 4 yards
  (3.66 m).
Waste wire, 20 gauge, contrasting color,
  ½ yard (46 cm).
2 gold end caps, purchased.
Size 8 (5 mm) knitting needle.
⅜" (1 cm) Allen wrench.
Drawplate.
Basic tools.

Note: Because this wire is so thick it is a bit more difficult to work with. The work has to be about 1" (2.5 cm) short of the desired length because it will not draw through the drawplate easily. It will only go through the first or second hole of the drawplate.

Using the basic Viking knitting setup (see Viking Knitting How-To, page 40) and 20-gauge waste wire, start with 5 loops. Join the gold 20-gauge wire and work chain for 5" (12.5 cm). Draw chain through the draw-plate to about 6" (15 cm). Cut away the waste wire; finish off gold wire ends by inserting them into the center of the tube.

Cut two pieces of gold wire 6" (15 cm)

long. ***For both ends,*** insert the end of a piece of wire into the end of the Viking knitting and wrap around the knitting. Place the end cap over the wire. You may have to reduce the size of the tip of the knitting by squeezing with the chain-nose pliers to make the caps fit snugly. Make a loop with the round-nose pliers and wrap the wire at the base of the loop next to the end cap. Work other end of chain the same.

Using the size 8 (5 mm) knitting needle and gold wire, make 1 jump ring (see How to Make Findings, page 9). Attach to one end of the bracelet. Make 1 hook of suitable size (see How to Make Findings, page 9), pound gently and attach to the loop at the other end of the bracelet.

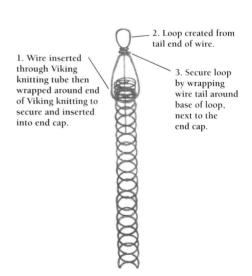

1. Wire inserted through Viking knitting tube then wrapped around end of Viking knitting to secure and inserted into end cap.

2. Loop created from tail end of wire.

3. Secure loop by wrapping wire tail around base of loop, next to the end cap.

Watchband

A simple beginner project.

Size

Length: 7½" (19 cm).

Materials

German Wire, 26 gauge, gold, 10 yards
(9.15 m).
German Wire, 18 gauge, gold, 18" (46 cm).
Waste wire, 26 gauge, contrasting color,
about 1½ yards (1.37 m).
Basic tools
1 watch with 3 holes for connection of
band, purchased.
1 clasp with 3 holes for connection of band,
purchased.
³⁄₁₆" (6 mm) Allen wrench.
Drawplate.
Size 6 (4 mm) knitting needle.

*Using the basic Viking knitting setup (see
Viking Knitting How-To, page 40) and 26-
gauge waste wire, start with 4 loops. Join
gold 26-gauge wire and work chain for
about 2" (5 cm). Draw through drawplate to
about 3 to 3½" (7.5–9 cm). Chain should be
firm. Remove the waste wire and weave the
main wire tails into the middle of the tube*.
Repeat from * to * 5 more times—6 chains
total.

Using size 6 (4 mm) knitting needle and
18-gauge gold wire make 12 jump rings (see
How to Make Findings, page 9). Attach all 6
pieces of knitting to the watch using the
jump rings (3 chains on each side of watch).
Be sure jump ring is securely fastened to
knitting. Lay out the watchband and measure the length plus the length of the clasp.
Adjust the length to fit your wrist by trim-
ming any excess from the ends of the knitting. Weave the ends of the main wire into
the center of the tubes. If you want the band
tighter so it doesn't slip around the wrist,
make the middle pieces slightly shorter.
Attach the knitting to the clasp with the
remaining jump rings the same as you connected them to the watch. Be careful that the
tubes of knitting aren't twisted when you
attach them to the clasp.

Silver Twist Bracelet and Necklace

Simply elegant basic Viking knitting.

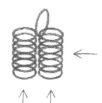

1. Wrap wire around knitting needle to make 15 loops. Fold in half with one loop in the middle (top) as shown.

2. Insert Viking knitting through the tube of loops following the direction of arrows.

Sizes

Bracelet length: 7" (18 cm) with clasp.
Necklace length: 16" (40.5 cm) with clasp.

Materials

Sterling silver wire, dead soft, 26 gauge, 8
 yards (7.32 m).
Sterling silver wire, 18 gauge, 1 yard
 (91.5 cm).
Waste wire, 26 gauge, contrasting color,
 about ½ yard (46 cm).
¼" (6 mm) Allen wrench.
Size 8 (5 mm) knitting needle.
Size 6 (4 mm) knitting needle.
Drawplate.
Basic tools.

3. Viking knitting inserted into wire ends.

Bracelet

Make two pieces.

 Using the basic Viking Knitting setup (see
Viking Knitting How-To, page 40) and 26-
gauge waste wire, start with 5 loops. Join
silver 26-gauge wire and work chain for
about 4" (10 cm). Draw chain through drawplate to about 6½" (16.5 cm).

 Remove the waste wire and weave in the
ends of the main wire through the center of
the knitting.

Clasp: *Wrap the 18-gauge wire around the
size 8 (5 mm) knitting needle 15 times (see

How to Make Findings, page 9). Cut wire.
Fold tube so that 7 wraps are on each side
and one loop comes out from the middle.
Loop a piece of waste wire into one end of
the Viking knitting. Insert waste wire into one
side of the clasp end (opposite end from the
center loop) and pull Viking knitting through
the clasp. Remove waste wire. Bend the tail of
the clasp into the middle of the tube to
secure. Attach the other end of the tube to the
other side of clasp in the same manner *.

 Repeat from * to * above with second piece
of Viking knitting with this exception—
before connecting second side of tube, insert

through the first loop of Viking knitting, linking both pieces together (figure 3), and then connect second tube to its clasp as described previously.

Using the 18-gauge wire and size 6 (4 mm) knitting needle, make 1 jump ring. Make suitable size S hook with 18-gauge wire and pound gently. Attach jump ring

and S hook to one of the loops at the end of the clasp.

Necklace

Make two pieces.

Work exactly as bracelet for 9½" (24 cm). Pull to 15" (38 cm). Finish closure same as bracelet.

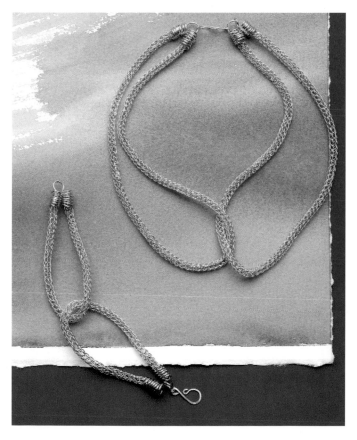

Cuffs with Scrolls

Viking knitting with fun finishing. Intermediate project.

Cuff One

Size
Length: 6½" (16.5 cm).

Materials
14-carat gold wire, 28 gauge, ⅛ ounces
(3.54 g).
14-carat gold wire, or gold-plated wire,
20 gauge, 1 yard (91.5 cm).
Waste wire, 28 gauge, any color, about
½ yard (46 cm).
⅜" (1 cm) Allen wrench.
Basic tools.

Using the basic Viking Knitting setup (see
Viking Knitting How-To, page 40) and 28-
gauge waste wire, start with 6 loops. Join
gold 28-gauge wire and work chain for
about 3¼" (8.5 cm); if you want a longer
bracelet add to this measurement. Cut 4
pieces of 20-gauge wire each 8" (20.5 cm)
long. Insert the four pieces into the tube of
knitting and secure them by wrapping the
waste wire ends around all four pieces. Carefully draw the tube with the wires in the
middle through the drawplate to about 6½"
(16.5 cm) in length. The large wires inserted
through the middle will not allow you to
draw through a very small hole. The tube
should be about ¼" (6 mm) in diameter.

Remove the waste wire, and check to make
sure the 20-gauge wires protruding from the
bracelet are of equal length at each end.
Wrap the ends of the 28-gauge gold wire
tightly around the ends of the larger wire.
Make scrolls (see How to Make Findings,
page 9) at both ends of chain with the ends
from the heavier wire. Hammer gently. Carefully bend the piece into a loose cuff that
will fit the wrist. It can be tightened slightly
when worn.

Cuff Two

Size
Length: 6½" (16.5 cm).

Materials
Artistic Wire, 28 gauge, silvered lilac, 1 yard
(91.5 cm).

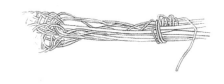

Artistic Wire, 20 gauge, fuchsia, 24" (61 cm).
Artistic Wire, 18 gauge, green, 20" (51 cm).
Waste wire, 28 gauge, any color, ½ yard
    (46 cm).
⅜" (1 cm) Allen wrench.
Size 8 (5 mm) knitting needle.
Basic tools.

Using the basic Viking Knitting setup (see
Viking Knitting How-To, page 40) and 28-
gauge waste wire, start with 5 loops. Join silvered lilac 28-gauge wire and work chain for
about 3½" (9 cm); if you want a longer
bracelet add to this measurement. Cut 2
pieces of green 18-gauge wire 9" (23 cm)
long. Cut 1 piece of fuchsia 20-gauge wire

9" (23 cm) long and 1 piece of fuchsia 12"
(30.5 cm) long. Insert the 4 pieces of wire
into the tube of knitting, and secure them by
wrapping the ends of the waste wire around
all 4 wires. Draw the tube and wires through
drawplate as described in Cuff #1. Remove
waste wire and wrap ends of silvered lilac
wire tightly around the larger wires on each
end. Make scrolls at both ends using the 9"
(23 cm) ends of wire. Hammer gently. Fold
the 12" (30.5 cm) wire ends over the Viking
knitting and using a size 8 (5 mm) knitting
needle wrap the wire around the needle to
create a curlicue. Trim the end so it won't
get caught on clothing or scratch your skin.
Carefully bend piece into loose cuff.

Viking Knit Covered Vase

Experiment with more stitches on a larger piece!
Intermediate and above.

Size

1½" (3.8 cm) wide at base × 5"
(12.5 cm) tall.

Materials

Artistic Wire, 26 gauge, aqua, 1 spool.
Size G/7 (4.5 mm) crochet hook.
Basic tools.
Purchased vase about 1½" (3.8 cm) wide at
the base and 5" (12.5 cm) tall with fluted
top.

Note: If you are unable to locate a vase similar to the one pictured, the directions are
easily adapted to any other round bottom
vase by working more or fewer single crochet to fit the base.
Base: With 26-gauge wire and crochet hook,

chain 4 (see Glossary for basic crochet
stitches, page 87). Join into circle with a slip
st. Work 2 single crochet in each stitch
around until base is slightly larger than bottom of vase. Join with slip st. Cut wire leaving a 24" (61 cm) tail, finish off.

Begin working a loose Viking knit stitch in
the top of each single crochet around the base
using the tail left from the crochet. Place the
vase on top of the crochet, using it as a mold
and work the stitches around it. As you work
up the side of the vase, tighten or loosen the
wire between the stitches to adjust to the size
of the vase. As you approach the top make
the wire between the stitches looser and looser to accommodate the fluted edge. Work
until the wire exceeds the length of the vase
by ½ to ¾" (1.3–2 cm). Be sure the wire
between the stitches goes over the top of the
vase to help hold it on. Finish off by weaving
in ends. You should not be able to remove the
vase once the knitting is completed.

Gold Bowl

A bit more work and the same Viking knit stitch for the advanced Viking knitter.

Size

4" (10 cm) wide × 2" (5 cm) tall.

Materials

German Wire, 20 gauge, gold, 2 yards
(1.83 m), for base.

German Wire, 24 gauge, gold, 1 package,
for body.

Ruler, or piece of stiff cardboard, 2" (5 cm)
wide.

Basic tools.

Small hammer.

An unopened soup can measuring 3⅛"
(8 cm) in diameter.

Wrap the 20-gauge gold wire 16 times around the 2" (5 cm) ruler as you would for basic Viking knitting setup. Cut the wire leaving a tail about 8" (20.5 cm) long. Gently remove the wraps from the ruler and insert the tail back through each wrap to the beginning, and form a circle. Twist the tail end to the beginning to secure the circle. Fan out the 16 petals and adjust so they lie flat to form the base of the bowl. Gently hammer the spokes of the base petals to

harden. Place on the top of the can. You will be working from the base toward the top of the bowl.

Cut about 2 feet (61 cm) of the 24-gauge wire and attach to center of base. Begin Viking knitting attaching the petals. The knitting should be against the can, and the petals should be coming out like spokes from the can. Adjust knitting to fit the diameter of the can. Keep the stitches evenly spaced and loose enough that the can is easily removed when finished. Continue working until bowl measures 2" (5 cm) or desired height. Work 3 more rows making the wire between the stitches progressively looser. Remove can and finish off piece by weaving in all wire ends.

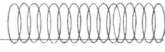

(a) Remove wraps from ruler and insert wire tail back through each loop.

(b) Twist wire into a circle to secure loops, then fan out loops into 16 petals to form base of bowl. Attach working wire to center.

Machine Knitting with Wire

History of Machine Knitting with Wire

I first discovered machine knitting with wire in Arline M. Fisch's book, *Textile Techniques in Metal*. She has created fabulous art jewelry using various techniques including knitting wire on a machine. I found this to be another fascinating technique to add to my knitting with wire repertoire. On my standard-bed knitting machine I tried to knit the wire smoothly and without breaking. The wire always broke before the pieces got very wide or very large. I was a bit discouraged, especially when I saw the work that Ms. Fisch was able to accomplish. I also discovered that there were limited types of wire in a gauge that would work with a knitting machine. I tried everything from electronic wire to wire from the hardware store. I wasn't having much luck with any of it.

At about this time wire working became popular in the bead world and manufacturers began to produce many gauges of wire in a variety of colors. Searching the Internet I learned that Artistic Wire Company was beginning to produce some 32-and 34-gauge wire that I knew was the perfect size for the knitting machine, but it was available only in copper. Now I was getting close to what I wanted, but I didn't want to knit everything

in copper. I experimented with adding colored rayon threads. Not only does the thread change the color of the wire, it keeps it from breaking! It also makes the wire feel softer and easier to wear, and the rayon and wire can be manipulated without breakage for flowers and sculpture, or to add shaping. I was thrilled at this discovery. Now I really was set!

Or so I thought, but after much trial and error, I have finally perfected my methods for working with the wire, and now I am successful 95 percent of the time. I still get breakage occasionally, especially with the cast on. But in general I am able to knit very large pieces without problems. And now I'm passing on my secrets to you.

Machine Knitting How-To

Using the box and dowel setup as described in the tools section, place the wire on the dowel with the wire coming off the back of the spool. Set the dowel in the box with ends cradled in the cut-out areas at each end. I use either a single or a double strand of Sulky Rayon thread in 40 weight for all the projects. Drop the spool of threads in the box, behind the wire. Holding the wire and the thread together, thread through the machine in the normal manner: through the mast and tension to the carriage. Set tension on carriage as directed in pattern; mast tension is set in the middle range. Pull the required number of needles out to D position.

Casting On

Cast on with a chain stitch using the latch tool: With the wire and the thread held together as one, make a slip knot and place on the latch tool, below the latch (Figure 1). Insert the latch tool from the bottom

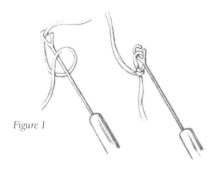

Figure 1

between the first and second needle on the left. All stitches should be made below the latch of the needles on the machine. *Holding the wire and thread in your left hand and the latch tool in the right, lay the wire and thread over the needle, bring the latch tool up, and catch the wire and thread with the hook of the latch tool, then pull the latch tool down through the slipknot to

create a chain stitch on the first needle (Figure 2). Bring the latch tool up through

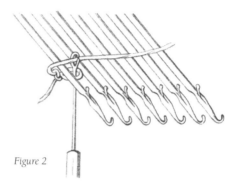

Figure 2

the space between the next two needles and repeat from * (Figure 3). Work the chain

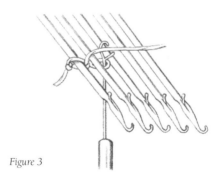

Figure 3

stitch loosely to keep it from breaking when the first row is knitted. When all the stitches have been made except for the last stitch, enlarge the loop on the latch tool and place over the last needle (Figure 4). Be sure the wire and thread go between the

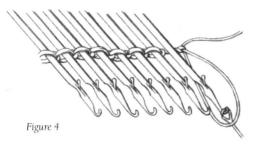

Figure 4

needles and toward the bottom when you place them in the carriage.

Knit the first row very slowly and carefully. It will be slightly difficult to push the carriage across the cast on stitches. Check the cast on row, and if the wire or thread has not broken, pull all needles forward so stitches are behind the latches; carefully knit the second row. If the threads or wire have broken, start over. If not, you're good to go. Gently place a single claw weight into the cast-on edge if the knitting is no more than 10

stitches wide; if it is more, place two claw weights, one at each edge. Proceed slowly and carefully, gently holding down the knitting with the left hand. Move the claw weights up about every 20 to 30 rows.

Tip

If you are having trouble knitting the first row without the wire or thread breaking, you are probably casting on too tightly.

Binding Off

Using the wire and thread held together, carriage on the right, knit the last row manually, creating stitches twice the normal size. Bring the needles out to D position. Cut the wire and thread. Leave one claw weight in the knitting about 12 to 15" (30.5-38 cm) below needle bed. Using the latch tool, crochet off the stitches working from right to left. Be careful to catch both the wire and the thread in each stitch. Finish off.

Machine Knitting Projects

Beaded Ties

A simple machine-knit narrow scarf—this project is for everyone, beginner included.

Note: Both scarves can be gently tied at the neck. Do not knot or crease. Store ties wrapped around a tube or round container.

Red Tie
Size
46" (117 cm) long × 1¾" (4.5 cm) wide.

Materials
Artistic Wire, 34 gauge, magenta, 1 spool.
Sulky Rayon Thread, 40 wt, #142 7014
    Christmas red metallic, 1 spool.
Size 10° seed beads, red, ½ tube.
Size 6° square beads, red, 21 beads.
Silamide beading thread.
Size 10 beading needle.

Using crochet cast on with both wire and thread held together, CO 12 sts. Place 2 claw weights. Knit 400 rows at tension 6, moving claw weights up every 20 rows.
    Manually knit last row and BO.

Finishing: Sew the end into a point by folding the corners toward the wrong side and toward the center like an envelope. Sew edges together with Silamide thread, anchor thread securely at point. String each fringe as follows: With Silamide threaded on beading needle, secure thread to knitting, then string on 12 seed beads, 1 size 6° bead, 1 seed bead. Re-insert beading needle through size 6° bead, then the 12 seed beads. Stitch each fringe firmly to knitting and weave thread through sts to next fringe placement. Attach 2 fringes at the center point of the tie and 8 more strands along each edge of the "V". Make 18 fringes in all.

Surface beading: With Silamide threaded on beading needle, secure thread to knitting

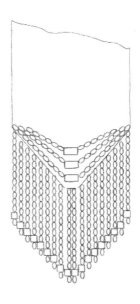

above the fringe; string on 10 seed beads, 1 size 6° bead, sewing the larger bead to the center point of the "V", above the fringe where the point of the tie is located; string on 10 more seed beads and anchor at top of fringe on other side. Repeat using 8 seed beads on each side and 1 size 6° bead in the middle, sewn just slightly above the previous row. Repeat using 6 seed beads on each side and 1 size 6° bead sewn in the middle across the top of the point. Work other end of tie the same.

Blue Tie

Size

50" (127 cm) long × 2" (5 cm) wide

Materials

Artistic Wire, 32 gauge, navy, 1 spool.
Sulky Rayon Thread, 40 wt, #942 1171
    weathered blue, 1 spool.
Size 10° square cut beads, blue 121 beads,
    silver 44 beads.
Large silver beads, ½" (1.3 cm) long,
    24 beads.
Silamide beading thread.
Size 10 beading needle.

Using crochet cast on with wire and thread held together, CO 12 sts. Knit 460 rows at tension 6.5, moving claw weights up every 20 rows. Manually knit last row and BO.

Finishing: Fold bottom edge to one corner, attach at side and top. *Fringe:* With Silamide threaded on beading needle, secure thread to knitting. String (2 blue and 1 silver bead) 4 times, 2 blue beads, 1 silver ½" (1.3 cm) bead and one blue bead. Re-insert needle through the silver ½" (1.3 cm) bead, then through remaining 14 beads. Stitch securely into the knitting. Repeat 11 more times, evenly spacing fringe across diagonal edge. Repeat for other end of tie.

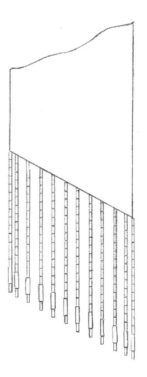

Copper Weaving

Basic strips of knitting woven around copper tubing shaped as a square. Beginner to intermediate project.

Size
13½" (34.5 cm) square.

Materials
Artistic Wire, 34 gauge, copper, 2½ ounces (71 g).
Size 18 tapestry needle.
From a hardware store:
Four pieces of copper pipe 1" (2.5 cm) in diameter, 12" (30.5 cm) in length.
Four 90-degree copper end pieces.
Epoxy glue.
Sulky Rayon Thread, 40 wt, 1 spool in each of the following colors:

WARP COLORS	STRIPS TO MAKE
142 7050 purple metallic	1 strip–15 sts wide
942 1545 purple accent	2 strips–11 sts wide
942 1533 light rose	2 strips–11 sts wide
942 1169 bayberry red	1 strip–15 sts wide
942 1109 hot pink	1 strip–15 sts wide

WEFT COLORS	
142 7015 jade green metallic	1 strip–12 sts wide
942 1208 mallard green	1 strip–12 sts wide
142 7052 peacock blue metallic	2 strips–10 sts wide
942 1177 avocado	2 strips–14 sts wide
942 1171 weathered blue	1 strip–10 sts wide

Glue the 90-degree copper end pieces to the pieces of pipe, forming a square. Allow glue to dry for 24 hours. Measure completely around the square to determine the length to knit for each strip, and add 1" (2.5 cm) for seam allowance—about 220 rows. Measure strips before BO.

Make all the strips listed above with machine tension set at 6. Using a crochet cast on with the wire and thread held together, and with the number of sts listed above, knit a strip the length you measured around the square plus the seam allowance. Manually knit the last row and BO.

After all strips are made, and using the tails of the wire and the thread held together, sew the ends of each strip together around the copper square in the following order. **Warp:** Starting at the left edge; purple accent, light rose, purple metallic, light rose, hot pink, purple accent, bayberry red. **Weft:** Turn the copper square to the side edges without warp; starting at the left edge, weave the knitting into the warp in a simple over-under pattern, over the outside edge of the copper pipe, then continue the weaving on the underside and sew the ends together snugly over the edge of the copper pipe. Use this order: peacock blue metallic, mallard green, avocado, weathered blue, jade green metallic, avocado, peacock blue metallic. Secure all ends and adjust weaving so it is evenly distributed over the copper square. Weaving can be hung from one corner or as a square.

Knitted Wire Box

A larger piece of machine knitting using Kitchener stitch to graft the seam together. Advanced project.

Size

4 × 5" (10 × 12.5 cm).

Materials

Artistic Wire, aqua, 1 spool.
Sulky Rayon Thread, 40 wt, #142 7022 jade/purple metallic, 1 spool; #942 1208 mallard green, 1 spool.
Size 10 crochet cotton in contrasting color.
Square box, 4 × 4 × 4" (10 × 10 × 10 cm).

With crochet thread, CO 40 sts using chain CO. Knit 6 rows at tension 6. Cut crochet thread. Using the wire and the 2 colors of thread held together, knit 160 rows, or until knitting fits snugly around box. Cut wire and threads. Using crochet thread knit 6 more rows. BO.

Using Kitchener st (see Glossary, page 87) graft the two edges together. Remove the crochet thread. Place tube over box and shape to box, creasing the corners gently with the fingers. Extend the knitting over the bottom of the box, so that when folded over the edge of the box the knitting meets in the middle. Sew the long edges together (Figure 1). Fold the points in and toward each other as though you are wrapping a package and sew down, this is the bottom of your wire box (Figure 2). Remove the box, pull gently on the top of the knitting to stretch, folding knitting outwards, to make it ruffle.

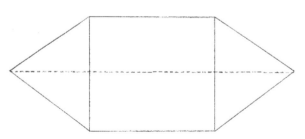

Figure 1

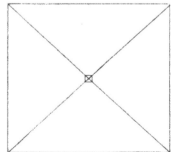

Figure 2

Fringed Necklace

A fabulous way to show off your skills and favorite beads with this advanced project.

Size
5 × 18" (12.5 × 46 cm)

Materials
Artistic Wire, violet, 1 spool.
Sulky Rayon Thread, 40 wt, #942 1545 purple accent, 1 spool.
Size 10 crochet thread, small amount in contrasting color.
1 clasp about ¾" (2 cm) square on both sides.
Size 11° seed beads, color to match, ½ tube.
Size 6 mm crystals, 23.
Size 8 mm crystal, 1.
Focal bead, color to match.
Nymo thread to match size D.
Beading needle.

Using Sulky thread and wire together, CO 3 sts at tension 6. Knit 2 rows.
Next row: Move a stitch at each end out one needle. Bring empty needles to working position, knit across—5 sts. Knit 1 more row. Repeat these last 2 rows until there are 25 sts.

Divide for center: Row counter at 000. Move center st one needle to the left. Move empty needle to out of work position. Hand manipulate remaining 12 sts to the left of center with crochet thread, BO. Move needles to out of work position. Cont with remaining sts as follows: *Dec 1 st at center edge every 4th row

and *at the same time,* on the outer edge every other row move the outside stitch in one needle, then move the 2 sts on that needle out one needle. Bring empty needle to working position, knit across and back. Repeat from * until there are a total of 6 sts. Continue knitting for a total of 100 rows, hand manipulate sts and BO.

Left side: Gently place sts that were bound off with crochet thread on needles. Repeat as above, reversing shaping. Weave in ends.

Focal Bead Fringe
With Nymo threaded on beading needle, starting one stitch to the right of center front, secure thread firmly to knitting. String on 20 seed beads, 1 small crystal, focal bead, large crystal and 3 seed beads. Re-insert beading needle through large crystal, focal bead, and small crystal, then string on 20 more seed beads and attach at opposite corner of center front. Sew 4 seed beads across the center front between the fringe attachments.

Side fringes: *Weave threaded beading needle up through the necklace stitches to the next yarnover hole in the knitting. String on 25 seed beads and 1 small crystal, 25 seed beads and attach firmly to knitting. Repeat from * for each hole up the sides of the necklace to where the neck was divided—a total of 11 fringes on each side.

Sew clasp to ends of necklace and finish off all ends.

Roses

Materials

Artistic Wire, 34 gauge, 1 spool. See individual project directions for specific colors.

Sulky Rayon Thread, 40 wt, 1 spool. See individual project directions for specific colors.

For roses on stems: Artistic Wire, 18 gauge, green, 24" (61 cm). For taller stems use longer length of wire.

Florist tape.

Note: All roses knit at tension 6.

Basic instructions for roses and leaves

Large Rose: About size 3" (7.5 cm) diameter, 1½" (3.8 cm) high. Using wire and thread held together, CO 15 sts. Work 60 rows. Dec 1 st at right edge, work 50 rows. Dec 1 st at right edge, work 40 rows. Dec 1 st at right edge, work 30 rows. Dec 1 st at right edge, work 20 rows. Dec 1 st at right edge, work 10 rows. With carriage at right, hand manipulate last row, BO remaining 10 sts leaving a 30" (76 cm) tail of thread. Cut the wire leaving a 6" (15 cm) tail.

Using only the thread through the tapestry needle, double and tie a knot. Turn the narrow end of the knitting toward you, wrong side up and *work a running stitch along the edge without decreases for about 1" (2.5 cm). Pull the thread to ruffle the knitting

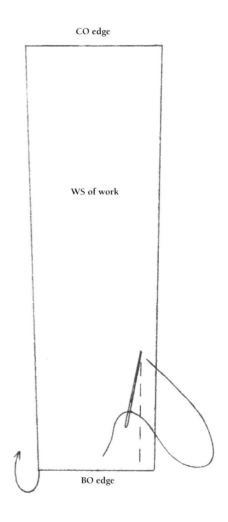

CO edge

WS of work

BO edge

ROSES OR BUDS WITH STEMS:

Colors shown: Red rose, Artistic wire, 34 gauge, red, stranded with Sulky Rayon Thread #942 1029 medium blue.

Two large leaves, Artistic Wire, 34 gauge, dark green, and one strand each of Sulky Rayon Thread #942 1176 medium dark avocado and #142 7027 multi-color in cranberry, gold, pine green metallic.

Red rose bud, same as rose with one medium leaf in same colors.

Dark rose bud, Artistic Wire, 34 gauge, magenta, with Sulky Rayon Thread #942 1533 light rose.

Single leaf, Artistic Wire, 34 gauge, natural, with one strand Sulky Rayon Thread #142 7010 dark copper metallic.

and pull into a circle, stitch in place to maintain shape. Repeat from * sewing down each small section. Keep the petals close together as you work, gently rolling the knitting into a spiral. Finish off. Gently pull on the outer edge of the flower to shape and enlarge. Tighten the center by giving it an extra twist. Sew the end of the knitting down to the outside of the rose when finished, if desired. Weave in all ends.

Medium Rose: About size 2" (5 cm) diameter, 1" (2.5 cm) high. Using wire and thread held together, CO 10 sts. Work 40 rows. Dec 1 st at right edge, work 30 rows. Dec 1 st at right edge, work 20 rows. Dec 1 st at right edge, work 16 rows. Hand manipulate last row, BO remaining 7 sts leaving a 26" (66 cm) tail of thread only. Cut the wire leaving a 6" (15 cm) tail. Finish as for large rose.

Small Rose: Using wire and thread held together, CO 7 sts. Work 24 rows. Dec 1 st at right edge, work 16 rows. Dec 1 st at right edge, work 10 rows. Hand manipulate last row, BO remaining 5 sts leaving a 20" (51 cm) tail of thread only. Cut the wire leaving a 6" (15 cm) tail. Finish as for large rose.

Rose Bud: About size 1½" (3.8 cm) diameter, 1" (2.5 cm) high. Using wire and thread held together, CO 15 sts. Work 50 rows. Dec 1 st at right edge, work 30 rows. Dec 1

st at right edge, work 20 rows. With carriage at right, hand manipulate last row, BO 13 sts, leaving a 24" (61 cm) tail of thread. Cut the wire leaving a 6" (15 cm) tail. Finish as for large rose, but do not pull on the edges of the knitting; leave bud as a tightly wrapped flower.

Make one or two leaves if desired to place on stem (see Leaves, page 79). Cut two pieces of green 18-gauge wire about 12" (30.5 cm) long (or longer if desired). Insert one piece into the base of the rose and bend the wire in half. Turn the rose a quarter turn, insert the other piece to form a cross with the first wire, bend in half and fold down (Figure 1).

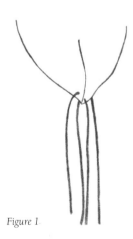

Figure 1

Begin wrapping florist tape at the top of the wire; be sure to cover base of rose. Place a leaf if desired about ½" (1.3 cm) below the base of the rose; holding the cast-on edge against the 18-gauge wires, wrap the florist tape over the leaf and around the stem (Figure 2). Continue to the bottom, fold the tape over the ends of the wire and wrap in the opposite direction for about 1" (2.5 cm).

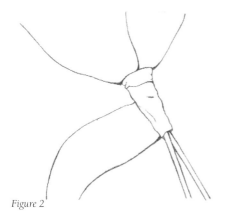

Figure 2

Note: Florist tape must be slightly stretched for it to stick to itself.

Leaves

Materials

Artistic wire, 34 gauge, 1 spool. See individual project instructions for specific colors.

Sulky Rayon thread, 40 wt, 1 spool. See individual project instructions for specific colors.

Large Leaf: About 2" (5 cm) long, 1" (2.5 cm) at widest section. Using wire and 2 strands of thread, CO 3 sts. Knit 4 rows. Using transfer tool, move the first and last st out one needle. Bring empty needle into working position each time a stitch is moved. Knit 2 rows. Move 2 stitches on each edge out, knit 2 rows.
* Move 3 sts out on each edge, knit 2 rows; rep from asterisk once more *. Knit 4 rows. Dec 1 st at each edge every other row, until 1 st remains. Finish off. Leaving a 10" (25.5 cm) tail of thread and wire, thread all tails through tapestry needle and weave up through the center of the leaf for support. Weave in all ends, or if being used on a stem, cover the ends with the florist tape.

Medium Leaf: About 1¼" (3.2 cm) long, ¾" (2 cm) at widest section. Using wire and 1 strand of thread, CO 3 sts. Work as for large leaf between * to *. Omitting the 4 knit rows, decrease as for large leaf. Finish off.

Rose Pin

A basic project for beginning rose makers.

Size
2 × 3" (5 × 7.5 cm).

Materials
Artistic wire, 34 gauge, magenta, 1 spool.
Sulky Rayon thread, 40 wt, #942 1183 black
  cherry; #942 1533 light rose; #942 1176
  medium dark avocado, 1 spool each
  color.
1 pin back.
Tapestry or sewing needle.

Following the basic rose instructions, page 76, make 1 medium rose using magenta 34-gauge wire, and 1 strand of #942 1183 thread. Make 1 small rose using magenta wire and 1 strand #942 1533 thread.

 Following the basic leaf instructions, page 79, make 2 medium leaves using natural 34-gauge wire, and 1 strand of #942 1176 thread. Sew the 2 leaves to the bottom of the large rose. Tuck small rose into end of outside layer of medium rose where knitting was cast on. With threaded sewing needle, sew on pin back.

Rose Necklace

Basic machine knitting—it's the finishing that's a challenge.

Size
24" (61 cm) long.

Materials
Roses and leaves: Artistic wire, 34 gauge, magenta, 1 spool; natural, 1 spool.

Sulky Rayon thread, 40 wt, Rose 1: #942 1533 light rose; Rose 2: #942 1074 pale powder blue; Rose 3: #942 1191 dark rose. 1 spool each color.

Leaves: #142 7011 light copper metallic, 1 spool.

Necklace: Artistic wire, 32 gauge, dark green, 1 spool.

Sulky Rayon thread, 40 wt, #942 538 forest green, 1 spool. #142 7027 multi-color combination of cranberry, gold, pine green metallic, 1 spool. One ½ to ¾" (1.3–2 cm) button for closure.

Drawplate.

Tapestry or sewing needle.

Roses
Following the basic rose instructions on page 76, make 3 medium roses using 34-gauge wire and 1 thread for each rose in colors #942 1533, #942 1074, and #942 1191. Do not cut thread after roses are sewn.

Leaves
Following the basic leaf instructions, page 79, make 3 medium leaves using 34-gauge wire in natural, and 1 strand of #142 7011 metallic thread.

Necklace
With 32-gauge wire and 1 strand #942 538 thread, CO 10 sts. Use tension 6. Work 210 rows. Change to #142 7027 metallic thread, work 210 rows. Hand manipulate last row and BO.

Gently roll the wire in the palms of your hands to make a tube, pull through drawplate to smooth. Fold in half at the color change, leaving a loop large enough for the button to go through. Sew base of buttonhole loop closed to maintain its size. Twist the two loose ends of the tube together and secure. Sew button to opposite end.

Lay the necklace on a flat surface. Find center front. *Gently open up the two strands of the necklace tube, placing the rose between the necklace strands and using the attached thread, sew Rose #2 firmly to necklace. Work all sewing stitches on wrong side of necklace and avoid exposing stitches on RS of rose petals *. Repeat from * to * 2 more times, positioning Rose #1 and #3 on each side of Rose #2. Sew the copper leaves to the back of the work as shown in photo.

Bridal Comb

More roses with basic finishing—beginning to intermediate project.

Size

3 × 5" (7.5 × 12.5 cm).

Materials

Artistic wire, 34 gauge, tinned copper, 1 spool.

Sulky Rayon thread, 40 wt, #942 1002 soft white; #142 7001 silver, 1 spool each color.

Clear plastic comb 3½" (9 cm) wide.

Ribbon ⅝" (1.5 cm) wide, 3½ yards (2.75 m), white with silver edges.

Sewing needle and white sewing thread.

Following the basic rose instructions on page 76, make 2 medium roses using 2 strands of #942 1002 thread, and 1 strand of tinned copper 34-gauge wire.

Make 1 medium rose as above using only 1 strand of #942 1002 thread with 1 strand 34-gauge wire. Following the basic leaf instructions on page 79, make 3 medium sized leaves using 1 strand #942 1002 thread, and 1 strand of #142 7001.

Weave in all ends. Sew loops of ribbon to comb first. Attach flowers and leaves using diagram for placement.

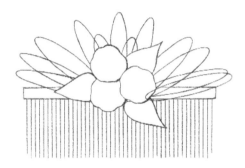

Flower Hat

Perfect large roses, easy to finish—advanced beginner to intermediate project.

Materials

Purchased straw hat.

Hot glue gun.

Artistic wire, 34 gauge, yellow, 1 spool.

Sulky Rayon thread, 40 wt, #942 1167 maize yellow; 942 1257 deep coral; 942 1259 salmon for roses; #942 1126 tan for leaves, 1 spool each color.

Following the basic rose instructions on page 76, make 3 large roses using the following combinations: Rose 1: 34-gauge yellow wire and 1 strand #942 1167 thread. Rose 2: wire and 1 strand #942 1257 thread. Rose 3: wire and 1 strand #942 1259 thread.

Following the basic leaf instructions on page 79, make 2 large leaves using wire and 1 strand #942 1126 thread. Hot glue roses and leaves to back of hat as shown below.

Glossary

Basic Crochet Stitches

Chain—Make a slipknot and place on hook. *Yarn over hook and draw it through loop of the slipknot. Repeat from * for desired length. To fasten off, cut thread or wire and draw tail through last loop formed.

Slip stitch crochet— Insert hook into stitch, yarn over hook and draw loop through stitch and through loop on hook.

Single crochet—*Insert the hook into a stitch, yarn over hook and draw a loop through stitch (2 loops on hook), yarn over hook (Figure 1) and draw it through both loops on hook (Figure 2). Repeat from * as many times as necessary.

Figure 1   **Figure 2**

Kitchener Stitch

Step 1: Bring threaded needle through front stitch as if to purl and leave stitch on needle.

Step 2: Bring threaded needle through back stitch as if to knit and leave stitch on needle.

Step 3: Bring threaded needle through the same front stitch as if to knit and slip this stitch off needle. Bring threaded needle through next front stitch as if to purl and leave stitch on needle.

Step 4: Bring threaded needle through first back stitch as if to purl, slip that stitch off, bring needle through next back stitch as if to knit, leave this stitch on needle.

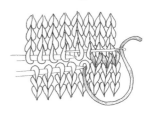

Repeat Steps 3 and 4 until all stitches worked.

Whipstitch

Insert needle at right angle through a stitch on one piece of the work, then through a corresponding stitch on the piece to be attached. Pull stitches together, closing both pieces firmly, but not too tightly.

Abbreviations

beg	beginning; begin; begins	rnd(s)	round(s)
BO	bind off	RS	right side
cm	centimeter(s)	sl	slip
CO	cast on	sl st	slip a stitch (purlwise unless otherwise indicated)
cont	continue		
dec(s)	decrease(s); decreasing	ssk	A single decrease. Slip two stitches knitwise, one at a time. Insert tip of left hand needle into front loops of both stitches from left to right, and knit them together in this position.
dpn	double-pointed needle(s)		
g	gram(s)		
inc	increase(s); increasing		
k	knit		
k2tog	knit two stitches together	st(s)	stitch(es)
kwise	knitwise, as if to knit	St st	stockinette stitch
m	marker(s)	tog	together
MC	main color	WS	wrong side
m	meter	yo	yarn over
mm	millimeters	*	repeat starting point (i.e., rep from *)
p	purl		
psso	pass slipped stitch over	* *	repeat all instructions between (i.e., rep from * to *)
p2tog	purl two stitches together		

Resources

Please shop at your local bead store for beads and findings. There are many bead stores in the United States. There are also many mail-order stores from which to purchase items on the Internet.

For a list of stores and advertisements consult:
Beadwork® magazine
Interweave Press
201 E. Fourth St.
Loveland, CO 80537-5655
www.interweave.com

For direct ordering consult:
Artistic Wire, German wire, and tools
Soft Flex Company
(707) 938-3539
www.softflexcompany.com

14-carat gold and sterling silver wire
Rio Grande
7500 Bluewater Rd. NW
Albuquerque, NM 87121-1962
www.riogrande.com

Purse frame
Bag Lady Bags
PO Box 2409
Evergreen, CO 80437-2409
www.baglady.com

Bibliography

Fisch, Arline M. *Textile Techniques in Metal*. Asheville, North Carolina: Lark Books, 1996.

Lareau, Mark. *All Wired Up*. Loveland, Colorado: Interweave Press, 2000.

Peterson, Irene From. *Great Wire Jewelry, Projects and Techniques*. Asheville, North Carolina: Lark Books, 1998.

Rutt, Bishop. *A History of Hand Knitting*. Loveland, Colorado: Interweave Press, 1987.

Untracht, Oppi. *Jewelry Concepts and Technology*. New York: Doubleday and Company, 1985.

Index